WILLIAM SHAKESPEARE was born in Stratford-upon-Avon in April, 1564, and his birth is traditionally celebrated on April 23. The facts of his life, known from surviving documents, are sparse. He was one of eight children born to John Shakespeare, a merchant of some standing in his community. William probably went to the King's New School in Stratford, but he had no university education. In November 1582, at the age of eighteen, he married Anne Hathaway, eight years his senior, who was pregnant with their first child, Susanna. She was born on May 26, 1583. Twins, a boy, Hamnet (who would die at age eleven), and a girl, Judith, were born in 1585. By 1592 Shakespeare had gone to London, working as an actor and already known as a playwright. A rival dramatist, Robert Greene, referred to him as "an upstart crow, beautified with our feathers." Shakespeare became a principal shareholder and playwright of the successful acting troupe the Lord Chamberlain's men (later, under James I, called the King's men). In 1599 the Lord Chamberlain's men built and occupied the Globe Theatre in Southwark near the Thames River. Here many of Shakespeare's plays were performed by the most famous actors of his time, including Richard Burbage, Will Kempe, and Robert Armin. In addition to his 37 plays, Shakespeare had a hand in others, including *Sir Thomas More* and *The Two Noble Kinsmen*, and he wrote poems, including *Venus and Adonis* and *The Rape of Lucrece*. His 154 sonnets were published, probably without his authorization, in 1609. In 1611 or 1612 he gave up his lodgings in London and devoted more and more of his time to retirement in Stratford, though he continued writing such plays as *The Tempest* and *Henry VIII* until about 1613. He died on April 23, 1616, and was buried in Holy Trinity Church, Stratford. No collected edition of his plays was published during his lifetime, but in 1623 two members of his acting company, John Heminges and Henry Condell, published the great collection now called the First Folio.

Bantam Shakespeare
The Complete Works—29 Volumes
Edited by David Bevington
With forewords by Joseph Papp on the plays

The Poems: Venus and Adonis, The Rape of Lucrece, The
Phoenix and Turtle, A Lover's Complaint,
the Sonnets

Antony and Cleopatra	*The Merchant of Venice*
As You Like It	*A Midsummer Night's Dream*
The Comedy of Errors	*Much Ado about Nothing*
Hamlet	*Othello*
Henry IV, Part One	*Richard II*
Henry IV, Part Two	*Richard III*
Henry V	*Romeo and Juliet*
Julius Caesar	*The Taming of the Shrew*
King Lear	*The Tempest*
Macbeth	*Twelfth Night*

Together in one volume:

Henry VI, Parts One, Two, and Three
King John and Henry VIII
*Measure for Measure, All's Well that Ends Well, and
Troilus and Cressida*
Three Early Comedies: Love's Labor's Lost, The Two
Gentlemen of Verona, The Merry
Wives of Windsor
Three Classical Tragedies: Titus Andronicus, Timon
of Athens, Coriolanus
The Late Romances: Pericles, Cymbeline, The Winter's
Tale, The Tempest

Two collections:

Four Comedies: The Taming of the Shrew, A Midsummer
Night's Dream, The Merchant of Venice,
Twelfth Night
Four Tragedies: Hamlet, Othello, King Lear, Macbeth

William Shakespeare

HENRY V

Edited by
David Bevington

David Scott Kastan,
James Hammersmith,
and Robert Kean Turner,
Associate Editors

With a Foreword by
Joseph Papp

BANTAM BOOKS
NEW YORK · TORONTO · LONDON · SYDNEY · AUCKLAND

HENRY V

*A Bantam Book / published by arrangement
with Scott, Foresman and Company*

PUBLISHING HISTORY

*Scott, Foresman edition published / January 1980
Bantam edition, with newly edited text and substantially revised, edited,
and amplified notes, introductions, and other
materials, published / February 1988
Valuable advice on staging matters has been
provided by Richard Hosley.
Collations checked by Eric Rasmussen.
Additional editorial assistance by Claire McEachern.*

Library of Congress Cataloging Card Number: 87-24100

ISBN 0-553-21295-8

Published simultaneously in the United States and Canada

PRINTED IN THE UNITED STATES OF AMERICA

OPM   0 9 8 7 6

Contents

Foreword   vii

Introduction   xix

Henry V
  in Performance   xxvii

The Playhouse   xxxiv

HENRY V   1

Date and Text   121

Textual Notes   123

Shakespeare's Sources   125

Further Reading   157

Memorable Lines   163

Foreword

It's hard to imagine, but Shakespeare wrote all of his plays with a quill pen, a goose feather whose hard end had to be sharpened frequently. How many times did he scrape the dull end to a point with his knife, dip it into the inkwell, and bring up, dripping wet, those wonderful words and ideas that are known all over the world?

In the age of word processors, typewriters, and ballpoint pens, we have almost forgotten the meaning of the word "blot." Yet when I went to school, in the 1930s, my classmates and I knew all too well what an inkblot from the metal-tipped pens we used would do to a nice clean page of a test paper, and we groaned whenever a splotch fell across the sheet. Most of us finished the school day with ink-stained fingers; those who were less careful also went home with ink-stained shirts, which were almost impossible to get clean.

When I think about how long it took me to write the simplest composition with a metal-tipped pen and ink, I can only marvel at how many plays Shakespeare scratched out with his goose-feather quill pen, year after year. Imagine him walking down one of the narrow cobblestoned streets of London, or perhaps drinking a pint of beer in his local alehouse. Suddenly his mind catches fire with an idea, or a sentence, or a previously elusive phrase. He is burning with impatience to write it down—but because he doesn't have a ballpoint pen or even a pencil in his pocket, he has to keep the idea in his head until he can get to his quill and parchment.

He rushes back to his lodgings on Silver Street, ignoring the vendors hawking brooms, the coaches clattering by, the piteous wails of beggars and prisoners. Bounding up the stairs, he snatches his quill and starts to write furiously, not even bothering to light a candle against the dusk. "To be, or not to be," he scrawls, "that is the—." But the quill point has gone dull, the letters have fattened out illegibly, and in the middle of writing one of the most famous passages in the history of dramatic literature, Shakespeare has to stop to sharpen his pen.

Taking a deep breath, he lights a candle now that it's dark, sits down, and begins again. By the time the candle has burned out and the noisy apprentices of his French Huguenot landlord have quieted down, Shakespeare has finished Act 3 of *Hamlet* with scarcely a blot.

Early the next morning, he hurries through the fog of a London summer morning to the rooms of his colleague Richard Burbage, the actor for whom the role of Hamlet is being written. He finds Burbage asleep and snoring loudly, sprawled across his straw mattress. Not only had the actor performed in *Henry V* the previous afternoon, but he had then gone out carousing all night with some friends who had come to the performance.

Shakespeare shakes his friend awake, until, bleary-eyed, Burbage sits up in his bed. "Dammit, Will," he grumbles, "can't you let an honest man sleep?" But the playwright, his eyes shining and the words tumbling out of his mouth, says, "Shut up and listen—tell me what you think of *this*!"

He begins to read to the still half-asleep Burbage, pacing around the room as he speaks. ". . . Whether 'tis nobler in the mind to suffer the slings and arrows of outrageous fortune—"

Burbage interrupts, suddenly wide awake, "That's excellent, very good, 'the slings and arrows of outrageous fortune,' yes, I think it will work quite well. . . ." He takes the parchment from Shakespeare and murmurs the lines to himself, slowly at first but with growing excitement.

The sun is just coming up, and the words of one of Shakespeare's most famous soliloquies are being uttered for the first time by the first actor ever to bring Hamlet to life. It must have been an exhilarating moment.

Shakespeare wrote most of his plays to be performed live by the actor Richard Burbage and the rest of the Lord Chamberlain's men (later the King's men). Today, however, our first encounter with the plays is usually in the form of the printed word. And there is no question that reading Shakespeare for the first time isn't easy. His plays aren't comic books or magazines or the dime-store detective novels I read when I was young. A lot of his sentences are complex. Many of his words are no longer used in our everyday

speech. His profound thoughts are often condensed into poetry, which is not as straightforward as prose.

Yet when you hear the words spoken aloud, a lot of the
language may strike you as unexpectedly modern. For
Shakespeare's plays, like any dramatic work, weren't really
meant to be read; they were meant to be spoken, seen, and
performed. It's amazing how lines that are so troublesome
in print can flow so naturally and easily when spoken.

I think it was precisely this music that first fascinated
me. When I was growing up, Shakespeare was a stranger to
me. I had no particular interest in him, for I was from a
different cultural tradition. It never occurred to me that his
plays might be more than just something to "get through"
in school, like science or math or the physical education
requirement we had to fulfill. My passions then were
movies, radio, and vaudeville—certainly not Elizabethan
drama.

I was, however, fascinated by words and language. Because I grew up in a home where Yiddish was spoken, and
English was only a second language, I was acutely sensitive
to the musical sounds of different languages and had an ear
for lilt and cadence and rhythm in the spoken word. And so
I loved reciting poems and speeches even as a very young
child. In first grade I learned lots of short nature verses—
"Who has seen the wind?," one of them began. My first
foray into drama was playing the role of Scrooge in Charles
Dickens's *A Christmas Carol* when I was eight years old. I
liked summoning all the scorn and coldness I possessed
and putting them into the words, "Bah, humbug!"

From there I moved on to longer and more famous poems
and other works by writers of the 1930s. Then, in junior
high school, I made my first acquaintance with Shakespeare through his play *Julius Caesar*. Our teacher, Miss
McKay, assigned the class a passage to memorize from the
opening scene of the play, the one that begins "Wherefore
rejoice? What conquest brings he home?" The passage
seemed so wonderfully theatrical and alive to me, and the
experience of memorizing and reciting it was so much fun,
that I went on to memorize another speech from the play on
my own.

I chose Mark Antony's address to the crowd in Act 3,

scene 2, which struck me then as incredibly high drama.
Even today, when I speak the words, I feel the same thrill I
did that first time. There is the strong and athletic Antony
descending from the raised pulpit where he has been speaking, right into the midst of a crowded Roman square. Holding the torn and bloody cloak of the murdered Julius
Caesar in his hand, he begins to speak to the people of
Rome:

> If you have tears, prepare to shed them now.
> You all do know this mantle. I remember
> The first time ever Caesar put it on;
> 'Twas on a summer's evening in his tent,
> That day he overcame the Nervii.
> Look, in this place ran Cassius' dagger through.
> See what a rent the envious Casca made.
> Through this the well-belovèd Brutus stabbed,
> And as he plucked his cursèd steel away,
> Mark how the blood of Caesar followed it,
> As rushing out of doors to be resolved
> If Brutus so unkindly knocked or no;
> For Brutus, as you know, was Caesar's angel.
> Judge, O you gods, how dearly Caesar loved him!
> This was the most unkindest cut of all . . .

I'm not sure now that I even knew Shakespeare had written a lot of other plays, or that he was considered "time-
less," "universal," or "classic"—but I knew a good speech
when I heard one, and I found the splendid rhythms of
Antony's rhetoric as exciting as anything I'd ever come
across.

Fifty years later, I still feel that way. Hearing good actors
speak Shakespeare gracefully and naturally is a wonderful
experience, unlike any other I know. There's a satisfying
fullness to the spoken word that the printed page just can't
convey. This is why seeing the plays of Shakespeare performed live in a theater is the best way to appreciate them.
If you can't do that, listening to sound recordings or watch-
ing film versions of the plays is the next best thing.

But if you do start with the printed word, use the play as a
script. Be an actor yourself and say the lines out loud. Don't
worry too much at first about words you don't immediately
understand. Look them up in the footnotes or a dictionary,

but don't spend too much time on this. It is more profitable (and fun) to get the sense of a passage and sing it out. Speak naturally, almost as if you were talking to a friend, but be sure to enunciate the words properly. You'll be surprised at how much you understand simply by speaking the speech "trippingly on the tongue," as Hamlet advises the Players.

You might start, as I once did, with a speech from *Julius Caesar*, in which the tribune (city official) Marullus scolds the commoners for transferring their loyalties so quickly from the defeated and murdered general Pompey to the newly victorious Julius Caesar:

> Wherefore rejoice? What conquest brings he home?
> What tributaries follow him to Rome
> To grace in captive bonds his chariot wheels?
> You blocks, you stones, you worse than senseless
>   things!
> O you hard hearts, you cruel men of Rome,
> Knew you not Pompey? Many a time and oft
> Have you climbed up to walls and battlements,
> To towers and windows, yea, to chimney tops,
> Your infants in your arms, and there have sat
> The livelong day, with patient expectation,
> To see great Pompey pass the streets of Rome.

With the exception of one or two words like "wherefore" (which means "why," not "where"), "tributaries" (which means "captives"), and "patient expectation" (which means patient waiting), the meaning and emotions of this speech can be easily understood.

From here you can go on to dialogues or other more challenging scenes. Although you may stumble over unaccustomed phrases or unfamiliar words at first, and even fall flat when you're crossing some particularly rocky passages, pick yourself up and stay with it. Remember that it takes time to feel at home with anything new. Soon you'll come to recognize Shakespeare's unique sense of humor and way of saying things as easily as you recognize a friend's laughter.

And then it will just be a matter of choosing which one of Shakespeare's plays you want to tackle next. As a true fan of his, you'll find that you're constantly learning from his plays. It's a journey of discovery that you can continue for the rest of your life. For no matter how many times you read or see a particular play, there will always be something new there that you won't have noticed before.

Why do so many thousands of people get hooked on Shakespeare and develop a habit that lasts a lifetime? What can he really say to us today, in a world filled with inventions and problems he never could have imagined? And how do you get past his special language and difficult sentence structure to understand him?

The best way to answer these questions is to go see a live production. You might not know much about Shakespeare, or much about the theater, but when you watch actors performing one of his plays on the stage, it will soon become clear to you why people get so excited about a playwright who lived hundreds of years ago.

For the story—what's happening in the play—is the most accessible part of Shakespeare. In *A Midsummer Night's Dream*, for example, you can immediately understand the situation: a girl is chasing a guy who's chasing a girl who's chasing another guy. No wonder *A Midsummer Night's Dream* is one of the most popular of Shakespeare's plays: it's about one of the world's most popular pastimes— falling in love.

But the course of true love never did run smooth, as the young suitor Lysander says. Often in Shakespeare's comedies the girl whom the guy loves doesn't love him back, or she loves him but he loves someone else. In *The Two Gentlemen of Verona*, Julia loves Proteus, Proteus loves Sylvia, and Sylvia loves Valentine, who is Proteus's best friend. In the end, of course, true love prevails, but not without lots of complications along the way.

For in all of his plays—comedies, histories, and tragedies—Shakespeare is showing you human nature. His characters act and react in the most extraordinary ways—and sometimes in the most incomprehensible ways. People are always trying to find motivations for what a character does. They ask, "Why does Iago want to destroy Othello?"

The answer, to me, is very simple—because that's the way Iago is. That's just his nature. Shakespeare doesn't explain his characters; he sets them in motion—and away they go. He doesn't worry about whether they're likable or not. He's interested in interesting people, and his most fascinating characters are those who are unpredictable. If you lean back in your chair early on in one of his plays, thinking you've figured out what Iago or Shylock (in *The Merchant of Venice*) is up to, don't be too sure—because that great judge of human nature, Shakespeare, will surprise you every time.

He is just as wily in the way he structures a play. In *Macbeth*, a comic scene is suddenly introduced just after the bloodiest and most treacherous slaughter imaginable, of a guest and king by his host and subject, when in comes a drunk porter who has to go to the bathroom. Shakespeare is tickling your emotions by bringing a stand-up comic on-stage right on the heels of a savage murder.

It has taken me thirty years to understand even some of these things, and so I'm not suggesting that Shakespeare is immediately understandable. I've gotten to know him not through theory but through practice, the practice of the *living* Shakespeare—the playwright of the theater.

Of course the plays are a great achievement of dramatic literature, and they should be studied and analyzed in schools and universities. But you must always remember, when reading all the words *about* the playwright and his plays, that *Shakespeare's* words came first and that in the end there is nothing greater than a single actor on the stage speaking the lines of Shakespeare.

Everything important that I know about Shakespeare comes from the practical business of producing and directing his plays in the theater. The task of classifying, criticizing, and editing Shakespeare's printed works I happily leave to others. For me, his plays really do live on the stage, not on the page. That is what he wrote them for and that is how they are best appreciated.

Although Shakespeare lived and wrote hundreds of years ago, his name rolls off my tongue as if he were my brother. As a producer and director, I feel that there is a professional relationship between us that spans the centuries. As a human being, I feel that Shakespeare has enriched my understanding of life immeasurably. I hope you'll let him do the same for you.

❖

There's no question that in *Henry V* Shakespeare eulogizes a great hero and monarch of England, calling him "this star of England" and sprinkling the play with liberal doses of praise for his achievements. But *Henry V* is interesting from another viewpoint: it is the one play where Shakespeare talks, through the Chorus, directly to the audience all the way through from the very beginning, and sets this great historical work almost entirely within his own playhouse. "Can this cockpit hold / The vasty fields of France?" he asks in the Prologue. "Or may we cram / Within this wooden O [the Globe Theatre] the very casques / That did affright the air at Agincourt?" He keeps urging the audience to think big, to let the words and the language take us beyond the limitations of time and place.

But this is only the beginning. At the start of each of the acts, the Chorus is used to give vivid descriptions. The Chorus to Act 2 tells us how people all across England were reacting to the news of the war with France: "Now all the youth of England are on fire, / And silken dalliance in the wardrobe lies, / Now thrive the armorers, and honor's thought / Reigns solely in the breast of every man."

The most beautiful of these descriptions, to my mind, is the Chorus to Act 4, which takes us to the two opposing armies encamped outside of Agincourt:

> Now entertain conjecture of a time
> When creeping murmur and the poring dark
> Fills the wide vessel of the universe.
> From camp to camp, through the foul womb of
>   night,
> The hum of either army stilly sounds,
> That the fixed sentinels almost receive
> The secret whispers of each other's watch.

This Chorus also contains some of Shakespeare's most beautiful lines about Henry, as he describes the young King walking among his troops on the eve of battle:

> For forth he goes and visits all his host,
> Bids them good morrow with a modest smile,
> And calls them brothers, friends, and
>   countrymen. . . .
> A largess universal like the sun
> His liberal eye doth give to everyone,

Thawing cold fear, that mean and gentle all
Behold, as may unworthiness define,
A little touch of Harry in the night.

And then Shakespeare rapidly switches to the battle—"And so our scene must to the battle fly"—thus ending this remarkable speech.

Though here he shows Henry as a noble warrior, Shakespeare is not content with an idealized portrait, here or anywhere. In the final scenes of the play, Shakespeare reveals a victorious Henry who is cruel and calculating in pressing his victory home. He is a tough negotiator, ruthless in the conditions he demands for France's surrender, bringing that proud nation to its knees without the slightest hint of compassion. One of his conditions, of course, is that the French King's daughter, Katharine, be thrown into the bargain; in a sense, she is just another city to him.

It's in this context that we must see the wooing scene. Katharine is more than just a charming woman to Henry; she is one of the fruits of war, and a necessary bond in the alliance between England and its defeated enemy. And so Katharine's resistance to Henry is more than just cute, it is inextricably wrapped up with the politics of the situation. When Katharine asks coyly, "Is it possible dat I sould love de ennemi of France?" Henry's reply makes it clear that he is playing for high stakes and will brook no resistance: "No, it is not possible you should love the enemy of France, Kate; but in loving me you should love the friend of France, for I love France so well that I will not part with a village of it, I will have it all mine."

This aspect of Harry as a ruthless negotiator influences how this scene should be played and viewed. We mustn't be taken in by its surface charm; there is a struggle for power going on here, and by showing it, Shakespeare deepens and enriches *Henry V*.

JOSEPH PAPP

JOSEPH PAPP GRATEFULLY ACKNOWLEDGES THE HELP OF ELIZABETH KIRKLAND IN PREPARING THIS FOREWORD.

HENRY V

Introduction

Henry V (1599) is Shakespeare's culminating statement in the genre of the English history play. Unlike the late and atypical *Henry VIII* (1613), which is separated from the rest of Shakespeare's history plays by some fourteen years, *Henry V* sums up the historical themes with which Shakespeare had been fascinated for an entire decade. The play, first published in a "bad" quarto in 1600, must have been written not long after *2 Henry IV*. To be sure, the play does not entirely fulfill the promise made in *2 Henry IV* to "continue the story, with Sir John in it, and make you merry with fair Katharine of France." Falstaff is missing. As before, Shakespeare apparently saw a grand design to his four-play sequence (which had started with *Richard II*), but improvised when he came to the writing of each part. Despite these minor adjustments in the overall plan, however, *Henry V* is clearly intended to bring to fulfillment the education of a Christian prince and to illustrate the arts of kingship Prince Hal had derived from his experiences in the earlier plays. In a sense, too, *Henry V* sums up the achievement of the English history play not only for Shakespeare but for other popular playwrights as well. The patriotic history play, born in the excitement of the Armada era (c. 1588), had nearly run its course by 1599 and was soon to be supplanted by other dramatic genres such as satire and revenge tragedy. Dark and complex political realities were already changing the buoyant mood in which the history play had been born: the aging Queen Elizabeth was near death and without a Protestant heir, while fear of another invasion threatened.

Henry V has become a controversial play, chiefly because its heroic king can, from the viewpoint of modern history, be looked upon as a warmonger and imperialist. George Bernard Shaw is prominent among those who have deplored Henry as a priggish and complacent chauvinist. Historically-minded critics have argued, on the other hand, that Henry is a perfect model of conduct according to Renaissance notions of statecraft and military leadership. What is Shakespeare's attitude toward his war hero? Does he sympathize with Henry's condescension toward the French and his ordering every soldier to kill his French prisoners? Or is Shakespeare's admiration qualified by ironic reservations? As is usual in Shakespeare's work, the perspective is complex and balanced. The play pulls us in two directions. Although the Chorus, who interprets the play for us, approves of Henry's military posture, the grandiose rhetoric of war is consistently undercut by matter-of-fact revelations of men's self-interested motives. This contrast between rhetorical illusion and political reality extends from the justification of Henry's French campaign to his state marriage with Katharine of France. The irony never amounts to open disillusionment in this play; it is instead the acknowledgment of a special kind of morality pertaining to kingship.

Skill in rhetoric is a key to Henry's success—in defying the French Dauphin, in preparing troops for battle, or in wooing the French princess for his queen. As the Archbishop of Canterbury notes approvingly, King Henry's versatility as a rhetorician applies to all the vital disciplines of kingship: Henry can "reason in divinity," "debate of commonwealth affairs," "discourse of war," handle "any cause of policy," and in all such matters speak in "sweet and honeyed sentences" (1.1.39–51). Through the arts of language Henry displays piety, learning, administrative sagacity, political cunning, and military intrepidity. Like the contemporary play *Julius Caesar* (1599), *Henry V* is concerned with techniques of persuasion. (The earlier *Richard III* is also a highly rhetorical play, though chiefly through the negative example of tyrannical behavior.) Yet however much we may be swayed emotionally by the rhetoric, we realize that the public figure of Henry V is a mask behind which we can perceive little. Only rarely do we glimpse the affable young companion of the *Henry IV* plays. King Henry has accepted the responsibility of playing a political role. It denies him a private and separate identity, even—or especially—in choosing a wife. And it complicates our task of assessing the sincerity of his utterances. Is he genuinely pious, or has he merely learned the usefulness of pious utterance in swaying men's hearts? What especially are his motives for going to war against France?

Shakespeare could have begun this play with the stirring scene (1.2) in which Hal, urged on by his advisers, issues a defiant challenge to the French ambassadors. Instead, Shakespeare treats us to a prior glimpse beneath the patriotic surface. It seems that the Archbishop of Canterbury, threatened with a bill in Parliament designed to take away the better half of the Church's possessions, has resolved to parry with a counterproposal, whereby the Church will give Henry a very substantial sum for his French campaign, provided the offensive tax bill can be conveniently forgotten. The Archbishop has already been negotiating with Henry and surmises that the plan will work. This revelation is not shocking to us; it merely reveals the political process at work. The faint undercurrent of anticlericalism suggests that Henry is to be admired for putting pressure on his clergy with such success; they are rich and can afford to support the war. In any case, the dramatic effect is to show how men's practical motives affect their rhetoric. When, in the subsequent scene, the Archbishop delivers a public lecture on the English claim to France, we know that this learned prelate has a prior and self-interested commitment to the war. His intricate dynastic argument, which he proclaims to be "as clear as is the summer's sun" (1.2.86), gives to the war a much-needed public justification. Henry's questions indicate not only his genuine concern about the legitimacy of his claim, but also his political need for the Church's endorsement of his cause; he has already claimed certain French dukedoms and must have the Church's official approval of those claims before he can proceed. He similarly needs the backing of his nobles, who also have their own reasons for approving the campaign. Henry skillfully orchestrates the scene to produce the desired effect of unanimous and patriotic consent.

Although never directly stated, Henry's own motives for going to war must also combine sincere zeal with calculated self-interest. As King, he longs to recover the French territory that England governed in the great days of Poitiers and Crécy. As a man, he bristles at the contemptuous challenge of the Dauphin; Henry must still strive to overcome his reputation as a wastrel and must prove himself worthy of honorable comparison with his great ancestors. Politically (and this motive remains most hidden), Henry has absorbed his father's sage advice to "busy giddy minds / With foreign quarrels" (*2 Henry IV*, 4.5.213–214), to blunt political opposition at home by uniting English resentment against a foreign scapegoat.

The exigencies of war do indeed provide Henry with an opportunity for proceeding against his political enemies. He arrests the Earl of Cambridge, Lord Scroop, and Sir Thomas Grey at Southampton on charges of conspiring with France. The scene (2.4) is, for Shakespeare, uncharacteristically one-sided. We are never even told that Cambridge is the chief pretender to the English throne, son of the Duke of York, married to Anne Mortimer, and founder of the Yorkist claim in the York-Lancastrian wars—the sort of rival whom Shakespeare elsewhere portrays with understanding. Instead, the rhetoric of the Chorus to Act 2 blatantly warns us to expect "hell and treason" (l. 29). These three conspirators, like Judases, says the Chorus, have bargained away their king for gold. (In fact, Cambridge insists that his motive was not financial, though he is not permitted to say what it was.) The playwright does not give them complex motives; they are sinners, so horrified by their own intents that they are actually grateful to be caught. The scene serves, by such rhetorical devices, to strengthen Henry's claim to the English throne as well as to the territories in France. Opposition to his rule during wartime is, in the view of the Chorus, simply treasonous; all persuasive evidences of dynastic rival claims are hidden from our view.

Comedy also contributes to the rhetorical image-making of the hero in *Henry V*. The tavern crew is on hand, though deprived of Falstaff's beguiling company and more distant from Henry than in the earlier history plays. Only briefly and in disguise, on the night before the battle, does the King encounter Pistol. The name of Bardolph comes to Henry as though in recollection of a distant past, when he hears that Bardolph is about to be executed for stealing from French churches. Henry confirms the sentence: "We would have all such offenders so cut off" (3.6.107). Whatever momentary pang Henry may feel, he remains constant to his banishment of Falstaff. And, although Shakespeare pleads for our sympathies in the seriocomic account of Falstaff's death, seen through the childlike naiveté of Mistress Quickly, there is no hope of reconciliation between Henry and his former mates. Pistol, despite his ornamental language, is little more than a boaster, coward, and thief. The tavern revelers are now the opportunists of war, troublemakers such as are found in every army, engaging rascals deserving to be cudgeled by more honorable men.

Pistol gets his comeuppance from Captain Fluellen, who replaces Falstaff as the chief comic figure both in prominence (his role is second in length to that of Henry) and in proximity to the King. Fluellen is a Welshman, like Henry of Monmouth, and is proud of this kinship. Because Fluellen is loyal and valiant, he is a person worthy to be seen in Henry's company. Yet there is none of the brilliant duel of wits previously linking Henry and Falstaff. Fluellen is a humorous character, identified at once by such comically exaggerated features as his Welsh accent and mannerisms of speech, his old-fashioned and somewhat fanatical sense of military propriety, and his devotion to the ancient rules of military discipline. Fluellen is a caricature, subject to mild satirical laughter, and there is a note of condescension in Henry's habit of playing practical jokes on the captain. (Henry makes practical jokes at others' expense as well, such as the soldier named Williams with whom he exchanges gloves.) Unlike Falstaff, Fluellen lacks perspective on his own pomposity. He is a zealot for duty, and one feels Henry is taking unfair advantage to pick on one who is such an easy mark for laughter. We suspect that Henry is using people again, bolstering his public image as the king with the common touch, borrowing a little Welsh color for myth-making purposes. At the same time, Fluellen is steadfast, upright, a credit to his countryman Henry. With his fellow captains from Scotland, Ireland, and England, he demonstrates that Britishers can fight together even if they do antagonize one another with their proud regional customs. Those customs are to be cherished as part of the British character; because Pistol offers gratuitous insult to the Welsh tradition of wearing a leek in the cap on St. Davy's Day, he must be thrashed.

As with the comic characters and Henry's political enemies, *Henry V* is rhetorically one-sided in its presentation of the French. Patriotism is a raw emotion, and Henry cannot appeal to it without awakening hostility toward the enemy. (Ironically enough, the great film version of *Henry V* by Laurence Olivier was created during World War II to arouse national feelings against the Germans rather than against the French, and with complete success. Any enemy will do in such patriotic moods.) The French are portrayed as haughty, vastly superior in numbers, envious of one another, contemptuous of their own leadership (especially the Dauphin), treacherous (attacking the boys with the luggage), and craven. Even their joking is characterized by an unattractively bestial kind of bawdry (3.7.48–68). The British—"we few, we happy few" (4.3.60)—are tired and outnumbered, but invincible and seemingly protected by God. Henry's order to kill the French prisoners and his description of the rapes and pillages his soldiers will commit if Harfleur fails to surrender (3.3.1–27), do, to be sure, raise serious questions about the morality of war under the best of kings; the play may be caustic toward the French nobility but does not necessarily exonerate the English. Even here, however, we are led to believe that, because the French are so execrably governed, France will suffer less under English rule. Henry takes care that his soldiers do not despoil the French countryside except under conditions of military "necessity." Only in Montjoy, the Duke of Burgundy, and Katharine of France does Shakespeare offer redeeming portraits of the French character, and in these instances the terms of hierarchical ascendancy seem clear: masculine English dominance, gentle French submissiveness. Katharine becomes "la belle France," depicted in Burgundy's eloquent peacemaking speech as being so much in need of competent management.

Henry woos Katharine with real flair, despite their unstated mutual recognition that their courtship is above all a matter of state in which they must play predetermined roles. The individual within Henry V gives way to the public personality, but he never loses his style. He manages always to be true to himself, as a wooer or as a soldier. We see him in disguise hobnobbing with common soldiers of his camp on the eve of battle, earnestly discussing with them the morality of war. We see him, with endearing human inconsistency, coveting all the glory of victory over the French and then adjuring his soldiers to give credit for that victory to God alone. Even if we are at times less attracted to this successful warrior and politician than to the carefree young man of *1 Henry IV*, we can still honor Henry's choice of responsible maturity and see that it is even compassionately self-denying. A king cannot be like other men, and Henry is willing to accept this price of leadership.

The Chorus presents *Henry V* to us as if it were epic as well as drama. Henry is an epic hero, defined in terms of mythic allusions and abstractions. He is compared to Mars, the god of war, with Famine, Sword, and Fire leashed at his heels, crouched and ready for employment. He is the "mirror of all Christian kings," and his followers are "English Mercurys" (2.0.6–7) with winged heels. Personified Expectation sits in the air, promising crowns and crownets to Henry and his followers. Henry's fleet of ships on the English Channel becomes "A city on th' inconstant billows dancing" (3.0.15). On the eve of battle, amidst his brothers, friends, and countrymen, Henry warms every heart with "cheerful semblance and sweet majesty" and with his "largess universal like the sun" (4.0.43). He forbids vainglorious pride and gives credit for his victory "Quite from himself to God" (5.0.22).

The action the Chorus describes is comparably epic, as it moves from England to France and back again, leaping over time, surveying all levels of society in the English nation, portraying famous military encounters seemingly more suited to epic narration (or to film) than to the stage. The stage's limitation forms indeed a major burden of the Chorus's argument. He apologizes to the spectators for the "flat unraisèd spirits" that have dared to bring forth so vast an object "On this unworthy scaffold," in this "cockpit" or "wooden O" (Prol.). The play confines "mighty men" "In little room," "Mangling by starts the full course of their glory" (Epil.).

This apology sounds like a becoming modesty on Shakespeare's part, in conceding the truth of Ben Jonson's objection that a few hired actors with rusty swords can scarcely do justice to England's great wars of the past. *Henry V* is not a Jonsonian neoclassical play. Paradoxically, however, Shakespeare's acknowledgment of the limited means at his disposal to create mimetic spectacle amounts to a defense of his own theater of the imagination. Through the Chorus's repeated urgings that we use our "imaginary forces" to supply what the actors and the theater necessarily lack, Shakespeare invites us as spectators and partners into his world of art. The play becomes a journey of thought, of making "imaginary puissance." When Shakespeare and his acting company talk of horses, we are to "see them / Printing their proud hoofs i' the receiving earth" (Prol.). This is not to minimize the importance of the theatrical experience, but indeed quite the opposite, since we are instructed to liberate ourselves through that theatrical experience and to recreate by means of Shakespeare's script an epic vision. Shakespeare's stage, bare of scenery, relying on good actors and the words they speak, becomes through its very flexibility more versatile in creating that vision than the most ornate and mechanically sophisticated illusionistic theater.

Henry V
in Performance

No Shakespearean play is more aware of its own theatrical limits than *Henry V*. Repeatedly, the chorus apologizes for the theatrical medium that requires us to supplement the spectacle before us with our imagination. We are asked to carry kings here and there on the wings of thought, to jump over long passages of time, to see horses when the actors speak of them, to make "imaginary puissance" by dividing each soldier into a thousand men, to see shipboys climbing the tackle of full-rigged ships at Southampton pier, to follow as the invasion army approaches Harfleur, to behold a siege there, to "entertain conjecture" of an army camp on the night before the battle of Agincourt with King Henry himself walking from tent to tent, to bear the King hence to Calais and London (where he is triumphally received) and back to France—in short, to "eke" out the performance with our minds. The Chorus speaks self-deprecatorily on behalf of his acting company and his author; the play cannot hope to "cram / Within this wooden O the very casques / That did affright the air at Agincourt," and so the actors must content themselves with confining "mighty men" in "little room," "Mangling by starts [i.e., in fits and starts] the full course of their glory."

Paradoxically, however, we grow increasingly aware that the Chorus is proud, not ashamed, of his spectacle and that his exhortations to us are a defense of a theater of imagination. All theater depends on synecdoche, that is, the part standing for the whole; the very essence of theater is illusion, to which an audience brings its understanding of the conventions by which theatrical signs are to be interpreted. This Chorus, in spelling out the conventions of Shakespeare's theater, places the emphasis where it rightly belongs, on our active participation in the reenactment or re-creation of the events that are being staged.

The original production of *Henry V* must have been spectacular in its own way, if only because it may have been the opener in 1599 for the company's new Globe Theatre.

Contemporary witnesses credit the London theaters of Shakespeare's day with being strikingly handsome. The conventions of illusion were, however, not verisimilar in the way the nineteenth century conceived of them, as we shall see. The original stage directions give clear hints as to staging. As the Chorus finishes the prologue to Act 3, for example, the text specifies *"Alarum, and chambers go off,"* suggesting that the stage action is supposed to mingle with the Chorus's final words. Then, *"Enter the King, Exeter, Bedford, and Gloucester. Alarum, [with soldiers carrying] scaling ladders at Harfleur."* The *Alarums* are forays onstage of armed soldiers; the *chambers* are cannon firing backstage. Much of the theatrical impression of warfare is conveyed by the sound effect of drum rolls and trumpet calls that the audience can readily interpret as signals of attack or retreat. The smell of gunpowder is in the spectators' nostrils, the sounds of war are in their ears, and before their eyes the theater facade now represents (without scenery) the walls of Harfleur. Scaling ladders are leaned up against the facade and used in breaching Harfleur's defenses. Spatially the theater provides a plausible three-dimensional locale for a siege, with fortified walls towering above the ground in front of them. When the Governor and some citizens appear on the walls in Act 3, scene 3, they are presumably in the gallery above the main stage, looking down on King Henry *"and all his train"* massing *"before the gates."* Clearly the acting company enlists as many extras as possible for this siege effort; their numbers are nonetheless symbolic, as they must be, even in the most epic of staging. The *gates* of Harfleur are represented by a door in the facade backstage, through which King Henry and his invading army exit from the stage, bringing to a close the military sequence at Harfleur: *"Flourish, and enter the town"* (3.3.58). Throughout, the theatrical emphasis is not so much on the military engagement itself as on Henry's ringing oratory and on the attempts of the irascible Fluellen to drive the reluctant Nym, Bardolph, and Pistol on into battle.

The early stage history of the play remains incomplete, despite these indications in the play script itself of how it was intended to be played. In 1605 the play was performed at court, and it seems to have been regularly acted at the

Globe Theatre. After the Restoration, it was infrequently produced. The diarist Samuel Pepys saw Thomas Betterton play in a non-Shakespearean *Henry V* in 1667 at the theater in Lincoln's Inn Fields, and it was not until 1738 that Shakespeare's play returned as a staple of the dramatic repertory. The Theatre Royal, Covent Garden, performed the play that year, and then in thirty-two of the remaining years of the century. *Henry V* was usually performed without the Choruses (though in 1747 and 1748 at the Theatre Royal, Drury Lane, David Garrick acted the Chorus), without Henry's arrest of the traitors in Act 2, scene 2, and without the soldiers' skeptical questioning in Act 4, scene 1. Dennis Delane, Sacheveral Hale, and Spranger Barry were among the finer eighteenth-century Henrys; Charles Macklin, Richard Yates, and Edward Shuter had great successes as Fluellen. John Philip Kemble first acted Henry at Drury Lane in 1789 and continued in the part until 1811.

On the nineteenth-century stage *Henry V* was regularly played, achieving a kind of monumental and costly splendor. By taking too literally the Chorus's appeal for visual effects, however, actor-managers often merely substituted verisimilar spectacle for the audience's imaginative participation. Set design undertook to supply, as far as was theatrically possible, all that was invoked by Shakespeare's poetry. William Charles Macready's production at Covent Garden in 1839, for example, hit on the novelty of accompanying the Chorus (spoken by John Vandenhoff in the character of Time) with a succession of pictorial illustrations executed by the painter Clarkson Stanfield. Act 3 began with a diorama that moved while the Chorus spoke, showing the English fleet as it left Southampton and traversed the English Channel until it came within sight of Harfleur. The action began onstage before the completion of the diorama, so that the picture melted, as it were, into the actual siege. Some enraptured spectators had difficulty telling when the diorama ended and the "real" action commenced. Samuel Phelps produced the play at the Sadler's Wells Theatre in 1852, striving, like Macready, for accurate and realistic visual effects, and succeeding in recreating English history in a theatrical experience that was, according to the *Morning Post*, "among the best things that the modern European stage has produced."

Charles Kean's 1859 revival at the Princess's Theatre attempted to outdo Macready and Phelps, with the siege of Harfleur realized onstage as literally as possible. Guns and engines of war that discharged smoke and flying stones were pointed at the walls of the town. Amid the confusion and din of war, King Henry, followed by seemingly countless soldiers, dauntlessly led the attack until Harfleur was reduced to rubble. In a similarly literal vein, Kean provided tableaux for the French and English camps on the night before Agincourt while Mrs. Kean (Ellen Tree), in the character of Clio, the muse of history, recited the Chorus to Act 4. Kean interpolated a crowd scene portraying King Henry's triumphant entry into London to accompany the recitation of the Chorus to Act 5.

Not until the twentieth century did directors attempt to recapture the fluidity and stage magic of the original script. Among recent productions, one that succeeds particularly in evoking the paradox of stage illusion is Laurence Olivier's film version (1944). Olivier places Act 1 and part of Act 2 in a reconstructed Globe Theatre in order to emphasize the limits and devices of theatrical illusion. We are ushered backstage to see boy actors filling out their women's bodices with pieces of fruit, or to see Olivier nervously clearing his throat before going onstage to a round of applause. The film condescends a bit to Shakespeare's theatre—sound effects such as striking clocks are late and require the intervention of the prompter (Shakespeare himself), and rain turns the open stage into a mire of wet hay in Act 2—but the point is well established by closeup shots that the actors wear makeup and are stylized in their Elizabethan dress. Having shown the way in which theatrical illusion is fabricated, Olivier then uses the camera to do what the theater cannot do, that is, show us the breathtaking gallop of horses across a French countryside (the sequence, in fact, was filmed in Ireland) and a flight of arrows toward the approaching enemy. When, at the concluding wedding of King Henry and Katharine of France, we suddenly find ourselves back in the Globe Theatre, we realize with a shock that the illusion has been contrived and yet wholly convincing. We accept the conventions of theater, while realizing that Olivier has been cheating by showing what we were to imagine. He has recreated the spectacle of

Macready and Kean, but with a theatrical self-awareness that aligns itself with Shakespeare's art.

Along with examining matters of illusion, stage history offers insight into the interpretation of Henry's character. Olivier's Henry—indomitable, brave and good-humored, unmistakably heroic and unabashedly English—was just the kind of patriotic tonic that war-wearied England needed in 1944. It was also recognizably part of a long stage tradition. Macready's and Kean's idealization of Henry as an invincible warrior had continued on into the early twentieth century in Frank Benson's many performances between 1897 and 1916; to demonstrate his prowess and fearless leadership, Benson as Henry pole-vaulted in full armor onto the walls of Harfleur. Lewis Walker (1900), not to be outdone by this sort of tireless athleticism, pushed himself off from a backstage wall just before his cue and thus arrived onstage at full speed for virtually every scene. Olivier played a heroic if restrained Henry in 1937 at the Old Vic directed by Tyrone Guthrie. In 1951, Alec Clunes, under Glen Byam Shaw's direction at the Old Vic, and Richard Burton, at Stratford-upon-Avon in a production directed by Anthony Quayle, each gave to Henry an interpretation that confidently stressed the play's patriotism and extolling of regal virtues.

Many recent productions, on the other hand, have explored the patriotism of *Henry V* with skepticism and, at times, open defiance. When Christopher Plummer played Henry in 1956 at Stratford, Ontario, with an attractive modesty qualifying his heroic energy, the production's most interesting political effect was achieved by its casting. Michael Langham invited French-Canadian actors from the Théâtre de Nouveau Monde to play the French roles, and in the context of Canadian politics the defeat of the French was no longer a simple patriotic triumph. Similar political concerns have shaped most recent productions. Certainly through the 1960s, the Vietnam War agonizingly forced a reappraisal of the play's insights into heroism and patriotism. The Royal Shakespeare Company's production in 1964 at Stratford-upon-Avon, for example, directed by Peter Hall, John Barton, and Clifford Williams, was a skeptical exploration of the realities of war, not the least part of which was its grimly realistic rendition of the Battle of Agincourt. Ian

Holm as Henry led troops who were visibly fatigued, enfeebled, their gayness and gilt all besmirched (as indeed the text calls for, 4.3.110). Theirs was the dogged heroism of trench warfare, of attrition, as one observer noted, "of men following a leader, not because he is a king, but because he is as tired and as stubbornly determined as they are." No doubt influenced by the Royal Shakespeare Company's production, Michael Langham again directed the play in 1966 at Stratford, Ontario, similarly focusing on war's brutality. Douglas Rain's Henry was impassively purposeful, showing no sign of remorse or even recognition when Bardolph's hanged body was dumped at his feet. Michael Kahn's Brechtian direction of the play at Stratford, Connecticut, in 1969, stressed even more overtly the antiwar theme. Hawklike bishops were shown manipulating Henry into an inglorious, imperialistic war that was then legitimized with the hollow rhetoric of patriotism.

Free of the immediate anxieties and tensions aroused by the war in Vietnam, recent versions have been more balanced, though still for the most part taking a disillusioned, antiromantic view of warfare. Terry Hands's production at Stratford-upon-Avon in 1975 was, as Hands said, "full of doubt." Alan Howard was a Henry always aware of the human costs of the war he must fight; his performance sought out Henry's self-doubt and showed the strain of overcoming it. At New York's Delacorte Theater in 1976, Joseph Papp directed an energetic *Henry V* with soldiers running helter-skelter across the smoke-filled stage, suggesting a war out of the control of any individual. In the final act, Meryl Streep's Katharine seemed ruefully aware that the ensuing marriage served Henry's political ambitions more than his romantic ones. *Henry V* returned to the New York Shakespeare Festival at the Delacorte Theater in 1984, directed by Wilford Leach with Kevin Kline in the title role.

Adrian Noble's direction of *Henry V* at Stratford-upon-Avon in 1984 revealed with unusual clarity what the play can be on the modern stage. On a drab open set designed by Bob Crowley, the play eloquently balanced its patriotic appeal with a full acknowledgment of the tawdry realities of war and politics. King Henry (Kenneth Branagh) eagerly wooed Katharine in the final scene even as the political negotiations earnestly continued, while behind a gauze curtain candles flickered on the graves of the soldiers who had died at Agincourt. If the complexity of the modern world insists that *Henry V* can no longer be played as an uncritical celebration of England's greatest medieval hero, it need not be taken to the opposite extreme as a harsh satire on imperialistic ambition. Without either glamorizing war or debunking public values, the play onstage, as in Noble's moving production, can effectively reveal the power of the heroic image that the play offers at the same time that it explores the physical, moral, and psychological costs of achieving that image.

The Playhouse

This early copy of a drawing by Johannes de Witt of the Swan Theatre in London (c. 1596), made by his friend Arend van Buchell, is the only surviving contemporary sketch of the interior of a public theater in the 1590s.

From other contemporary evidence, including the stage directions and dialogue of Elizabethan plays, we can surmise that the various public theaters where Shakespeare's plays were produced (the Theatre, the Curtain, the Globe) resembled the Swan in many important particulars, though there must have been some variations as well. The public playhouses were essentially round, or polygonal, and open to the sky, forming an acting arena approximately 70 feet in diameter; they did not have a large curtain with which to open and close a scene, such as we see today in opera and some traditional theater. A platform measuring approximately 43 feet across and 27 feet deep, referred to in the de Witt drawing as the *proscaenium*, projected into the yard, *planities sive arena*. The roof, *tectum*, above the stage and supported by two pillars, could contain machinery for ascents and descents, as were required in several of Shakespeare's late plays. Above this roof was a hut, shown in the drawing with a flag flying atop it and a trumpeter at its door announcing the performance of a play. The underside of the stage roof, called the heavens, was usually richly decorated with symbolic figures of the sun, the moon, and the constellations. The platform stage stood at a height of 5½ feet or so above the yard, providing room under the stage for underworldly effects. A trapdoor, which is not visible in this drawing, gave access to the space below.

The structure at the back of the platform (labeled *mimorum aedes*), known as the tiring-house because it was the actors' attiring (dressing) space, featured at least two doors, as shown here. Some theaters seem to have also had a discovery space, or curtained recessed alcove, perhaps between the two doors—in which Falstaff could have hidden from the sheriff (*1 Henry IV*, 2.4) or Polonius could have eavesdropped on Hamlet and his mother (*Hamlet*, 3.4). This discovery space probably gave the actors a means of access to and from the tiring-house. Curtains may also have been hung in front of the stage doors on occasion. The de Witt drawing shows a gallery above the doors that extends across the back and evidently contains spectators. On occasions when action "above" demanded the use of this space, as when Juliet appears at her "window" (*Romeo and Juliet*, 2.2 and 3.5), the gallery seems to have been used by the actors, but large scenes there were impractical.

The three-tiered auditorium is perhaps best described by Thomas Platter, a visitor to London in 1599 who saw on that occasion Shakespeare's *Julius Caesar* performed at the Globe:

> The playhouses are so constructed that they play on a raised platform, so that everyone has a good view. There are different galleries and places [*orchestra, sedilia, porticus*], however, where the seating is better and more comfortable and therefore more expensive. For whoever cares to stand below only pays one English penny, but if he wishes to sit, he enters by another door [*ingressus*] and pays another penny, while if he desires to sit in the most comfortable seats, which are cushioned, where he not only sees everything well but can also be seen, then he pays yet another English penny at another door. And during the performance food and drink are carried round the audience, so that for what one cares to pay one may also have refreshment.

Scenery was not used, though the theater building itself was handsome enough to invoke a feeling of order and hierarchy that lent itself to the splendor and pageantry onstage. Portable properties, such as thrones, stools, tables, and beds, could be carried or thrust on as needed. In the scene pictured here by de Witt, a lady on a bench, attended perhaps by her waiting-gentlewoman, receives the address of a male figure. If Shakespeare had written *Twelfth Night* by 1596 for performance at the Swan, we could imagine Malvolio appearing like this as he bows before the Countess Olivia and her gentlewoman, Maria.

HENRY V

[*Dramatis Personae*

CHORUS

KING HENRY THE FIFTH
HUMPHREY, DUKE OF GLOUCESTER,⎫
JOHN, DUKE OF BEDFORD,   ⎬ *the King's brothers*
DUKE OF CLARENCE,   ⎭
DUKE OF EXETER, *the King's uncle*
DUKE OF YORK, *the King's cousin*
EARL OF SALISBURY
EARL OF WESTMORLAND
EARL OF WARWICK
EARL OF HUNTINGDON

ARCHBISHOP OF CANTERBURY
BISHOP OF ELY

RICHARD, EARL OF CAMBRIDGE,   ⎫
HENRY, LORD SCROOP OF MASHAM,   ⎬ *conspirators against the King*
SIR THOMAS GREY,   ⎭

SIR THOMAS ERPINGHAM, ⎫
CAPTAIN GOWER,   ⎪
CAPTAIN FLUELLEN,   ⎬ *officers in the King's army*
CAPTAIN MACMORRIS,   ⎪
CAPTAIN JAMY,   ⎭
JOHN BATES,   ⎫
ALEXANDER COURT,   ⎬ *soldiers in the King's army*
MICHAEL WILLIAMS,   ⎭
An English HERALD

PISTOL,   ⎫
NYM,   ⎬ *Falstaff's former tavern-mates*
BARDOLPH, ⎭
BOY, *formerly Falstaff's page*
HOSTESS, *formerly Mistress Quickly, now married to Pistol*

DUKE OF BURGUNDY

FRENCH KING, *Charles the Sixth*
QUEEN ISABEL *of France*
DAUPHIN, *Lewis*
KATHARINE, *Princess of France*
ALICE, *a lady attending Katharine*
DUKE OF ORLEANS
DUKE OF BERRI
DUKE OF BOURBON
DUKE OF BRITTANY
CONSTABLE OF FRANCE
LORD RAMBURES
LORD GRANDPRÉ
GOVERNOR OF HARFLEUR
MONSIEUR LE FER, *a French soldier*
MONTJOY, *the French herald*
French AMBASSADORS *to England*

Lords, Ladies, Officers, Soldiers, Citizens, Messengers, and Attendants

SCENE: *England, afterwards France*]

Prologue

Enter [Chorus as] Prologue.

CHORUS

O, for a Muse of fire, that would ascend	1
The brightest heaven of invention!	2
A kingdom for a stage, princes to act,	
And monarchs to behold the swelling scene!	4
Then should the warlike Harry, like himself,	5
Assume the port of Mars; and at his heels,	6
Leashed in like hounds, should famine, sword, and fire	
Crouch for employment. But pardon, gentles all,	8
The flat unraisèd spirits that hath dared	9
On this unworthy scaffold to bring forth	10
So great an object. Can this cockpit hold	11
The vasty fields of France? Or may we cram	12
Within this wooden O the very casques	13
That did affright the air at Agincourt?	
O, pardon! Since a crooked figure may	15
Attest in little place a million;	16
And let us, ciphers to this great account,	17
On your imaginary forces work.	18
Suppose within the girdle of these walls	
Are now confined two mighty monarchies,	
Whose high uprearèd and abutting fronts	21
The perilous narrow ocean parts asunder.	22
Piece out our imperfections with your thoughts:	
Into a thousand parts divide one man,	
And make imaginary puissance.	25

Prologue.
1 Muse of fire (Of the four elements, earth, air, fire, and water, fire is the most sublime and mounting.)   **2 invention** poetic imagination   **4 swelling** splendid, magnificent   **5 like himself** i.e., presented in a fashion worthy of so great a king   **6 port** bearing   **8 gentles** gentlemen and gentlewomen   **9 flat unraised** uninspired, lifeless.   **spirits** i.e., actors and playwright   **10 scaffold** stage   **11 cockpit** (Elizabethan theaters were shaped rather like arenas for animal fighting.)   **12 vasty** vast, spacious   **13 O** (Refers to a round theater such as the Globe; the play may have been performed at the Curtain Theater.)   **casques** helmets   **15 crooked figure** cipher or zero (which, added to a number, will multiply its value tenfold)   **16 Attest** stand for   **17 account** (1) sum total (continuing the metaphor of *crooked figure*) (2) story   **18 imaginary forces** forces of imagination   **21 abutting** touching, bordering.   **fronts** frontiers, i.e., the cliffs of Dover and Calais   **22 perilous ... ocean** i.e., English Channel   **25 puissance** armed might, army

Think, when we talk of horses, that you see them
Printing their proud hoofs i' the receiving earth.
For 'tis your thoughts that now must deck our kings,   28
Carry them here and there, jumping o'er times,
Turning th' accomplishment of many years
Into an hourglass—for the which supply,   31
Admit me Chorus to this history,
Who, Prologue-like, your humble patience pray,
Gently to hear, kindly to judge, our play.   *Exit.*

28 deck dress, adorn   **31 the which supply** which service

1.1   *Enter the two bishops, [the Archbishop] of Canterbury and [the Bishop of] Ely.*

CANTERBURY
My lord, I'll tell you. That self bill is urged   1
Which in th' eleventh year of the last king's reign
Was like, and had indeed against us passed,   3
But that the scambling and unquiet time   4
Did push it out of farther question.   5

ELY
But how, my lord, shall we resist it now?

CANTERBURY
It must be thought on. If it pass against us,
We lose the better half of our possession.
For all the temporal lands which men devout   9
By testament have given to the Church
Would they strip from us, being valued thus:
As much as would maintain, to the King's honor,
Full fifteen earls and fifteen hundred knights,
Six thousand and two hundred good esquires,   14
And, to relief of lazars and weak age   15
Of indigent faint souls past corporal toil,   16
A hundred almshouses right well supplied;
And to the coffers of the King besides
A thousand pounds by th' year. Thus runs the bill.

ELY   This would drink deep.

CANTERBURY   'Twould drink the cup and all.

ELY   But what prevention?

CANTERBURY
The King is full of grace and fair regard.

ELY
And a true lover of the holy Church.

CANTERBURY
The courses of his youth promised it not.
The breath no sooner left his father's body
But that his wildness, mortified in him,   27
Seemed to die too; yea, at that very moment

1.1. Location: England. The royal court.
1 self same   3 like likely (to have passed)   4 scambling unsettled
5 question consideration   9 temporal used for secular purposes
14 esquires members of the gentry, ranking just below knights
15 lazars lepers   16 corporal physical   27 mortified killed

Consideration like an angel came   29
And whipped th' offending Adam out of him,   30
Leaving his body as a paradise
T' envelop and contain celestial spirits.
Never was such a sudden scholar made;
Never came reformation in a flood
With such a heady currance, scouring faults;   35
Nor never Hydra-headed willfulness   36
So soon did lose his seat, and all at once,   37
As in this king.
ELY   We are blessed in the change.
CANTERBURY
Hear him but reason in divinity,   39
And, all-admiring, with an inward wish
You would desire the King were made a prelate.   41
Hear him debate of commonwealth affairs,
You would say it hath been all in all his study.
List his discourse of war, and you shall hear   44
A fearful battle rendered you in music.   45
Turn him to any cause of policy,   46
The Gordian knot of it he will unloose,   47
Familiar as his garter, that, when he speaks,   48
The air, a chartered libertine, is still,   49
And the mute wonder lurketh in men's ears   50
To steal his sweet and honeyed sentences;   51
So that the art and practic part of life   52
Must be the mistress to this theoric.   53
Which is a wonder how His Grace should glean it,
Since his addiction was to courses vain,   55

29 Consideration meditation, reflection   **30 offending Adam** original
sin   **35 heady currance** headlong current   **36 Hydra-headed** i.e., many-
headed. (Alludes to the Lernaean Hydra, a monster of many heads
overcome by Hercules.)   **37 his seat** its throne   **39 divinity** theological
matters   **41 prelate** ecclesiastical dignitary   **44 List** listen to
45 rendered . . . music i.e., eloquently narrated   **46 cause of policy**
matter of statecraft   **47 Gordian knot** (It was foretold that whoever
should untie the Gordian knot would rule Asia. Alexander solved the
problem by cutting the knot.)   **48 Familiar** as offhandedly or rou-
tinely.   **that** so that   **49 chartered libertine** licensed freeman, able to
roam at will   **50 the . . . ears** i.e., wonder makes men silent, eagerly
listening   **51 To . . . sentences** i.e., to hear more of his sweetly profitable
wise sayings   **52–53 So . . . theoric** so that experience in practical life
must have been the teacher by which he acquired his theoretical conception   **55 addiction** inclination

His companies unlettered, rude, and shallow, 56
His hours filled up with riots, banquets, sports, 57
And never noted in him any study,
Any retirement, any sequestration
From open haunts and popularity. 60

ELY
The strawberry grows underneath the nettle,
And wholesome berries thrive and ripen best
Neighbored by fruit of baser quality;
And so the Prince obscured his contemplation
Under the veil of wildness, which, no doubt,
Grew like the summer grass, fastest by night,
Unseen, yet crescive in his faculty. 67

CANTERBURY
It must be so, for miracles are ceased. 68
And therefore we must needs admit the means 69
How things are perfected.

ELY   But, my good lord,
How now for mitigation of this bill
Urged by the Commons? Doth His Majesty
Incline to it, or no?

CANTERBURY   He seems indifferent, 73
Or rather swaying more upon our part
Than cherishing th' exhibiters against us; 75
For I have made an offer to His Majesty,
Upon our spiritual convocation 77
And in regard of causes now in hand, 78
Which I have opened to His Grace at large, 79
As touching France, to give a greater sum
Than ever at one time the clergy yet
Did to his predecessors part withal. 82

ELY
How did this offer seem received, my lord?

CANTERBURY
With good acceptance of His Majesty,

56 **companies** companions. **rude** coarse 57 **sports** amusements
60 **open . . . popularity** places of public resort and low company
67 **crescive . . . faculty** naturally inclined to grow 68 **miracles are ceased**
(Protestants believed that no miracles occurred after the revelation of
Christ.) 69 **means** i.e., natural causes 73 **indifferent** unbiased
75 **exhibiters** those who introduce bills in Parliament 77 **Upon** on behalf
of. **convocation** formal assembly of the clergy 78 **in hand** under consideration 79 **opened** expounded. **at large** in full 82 **withal** with

Save that there was not time enough to hear,
As I perceived His Grace would fain have done,   86
The severals and unhidden passages   87
Of his true titles to some certain dukedoms,
And generally to the crown and seat of France,   89
Derived from Edward, his great-grandfather.   90

ELY
What was th' impediment that broke this off?

CANTERBURY
The French ambassador upon that instant
Craved audience; and the hour I think is come
To give him hearing. Is it four o'clock?

ELY   It is.

CANTERBURY
Then go we in to know his embassy,   96
Which I could with a ready guess declare
Before the Frenchman speak a word of it.

ELY
I'll wait upon you, and I long to hear it.   *Exeunt.*

❖

1.2   *Enter the King, Humphrey [Duke of*
           Gloucester], Bedford, Clarence, Warwick,
           Westmorland, and Exeter [with attendants].

KING
Where is my gracious lord of Canterbury?

EXETER
Not here in presence.

KING   Send for him, good uncle.

WESTMORLAND
Shall we call in th' ambassador, my liege?

KING
Not yet, my cousin. We would be resolved,   4
Before we hear him, of some things of weight

---

86 fain gladly   **87 severals** details.   **unhidden passages** obvious lines of
descent   **89 seat** throne   **90 Edward** i.e., Edward III   **96 embassy**
message

1.2. Location: England. The royal court.
4 cousin (Correct form of address from royal family to nobles.)   **be
resolved** come to a decision

That task our thoughts, concerning us and France.   6

Enter two bishops, [*the Archbishop of Canterbury and the Bishop of Ely*].

CANTERBURY
God and his angels guard your sacred throne,
And make you long become it!

KING   Sure we thank you.   8
My learnèd lord, we pray you to proceed,
And justly and religiously unfold
Why the law Salic that they have in France
Or should or should not bar us in our claim.   12
And God forbid, my dear and faithful lord,
That you should fashion, wrest, or bow your reading,
Or nicely charge your understanding soul   15
With opening titles miscreate, whose right   16
Suits not in native colors with the truth;   17
For God doth know how many now in health
Shall drop their blood in approbation   19
Of what your reverence shall incite us to.
Therefore take heed how you impawn our person,   21
How you awake our sleeping sword of war.
We charge you in the name of God take heed;
For never two such kingdoms did contend
Without much fall of blood, whose guiltless drops
Are every one a woe, a sore complaint   26
'Gainst him whose wrongs gives edge unto the swords   27
That makes such waste in brief mortality.   28
Under this conjuration speak, my lord;   29
For we will hear, note, and believe in heart
That what you speak is in your conscience washed
As pure as sin with baptism.

CANTERBURY
Then hear me, gracious sovereign, and you peers,
That owe yourselves, your lives, and services

6 task engage, occupy **8 become** adorn, grace **12 Or** either **15 nicely
charge** subtly and foolishly burden **16 opening titles miscreate** ex-
pounding spurious claims **17 Suits . . . colors** i.e., does not naturally
harmonize **19 approbation** support, proof **21 impawn** pledge **26 woe**
grievance. **sore** severe, grievous **27 wrongs** wrongdoings **28 in brief
mortality** i.e., among mortal, short-lived men **29 conjuration** solemn
adjuration

To this imperial throne. There is no bar
To make against Your Highness' claim to France
But this, which they produce from Pharamond: 37
"In terram Salicam mulieres ne succedant,"
"No woman shall succeed in Salic land."
Which Salic land the French unjustly gloze   40
To be the realm of France, and Pharamond
The founder of this law and female bar.
Yet their own authors faithfully affirm
That the land Salic is in Germany,
Between the floods of Saale and of Elbe;   45
Where Charles the Great, having subdued the Saxons,   46
There left behind and settled certain French,
Who, holding in disdain the German women
For some dishonest manners of their life,   49
Established then this law: to wit, no female
Should be inheritrix in Salic land—
Which Salic, as I said, twixt Elbe and Saale,
Is at this day in Germany called Meissen.
Then doth it well appear the Salic law
Was not devisèd for the realm of France;
Nor did the French possess the Salic land
Until four hundred one-and-twenty years
After defunction of King Pharamond,   58
Idly supposed the founder of this law,   59
Who died within the year of our redemption
Four hundred twenty-six; and Charles the Great
Subdued the Saxons, and did seat the French
Beyond the River Saale, in the year
Eight hundred five. Besides, their writers say,
King Pepin, which deposèd Childeric,   65
Did, as heir general, being descended   66
Of Blithild, which was daughter to King Clothair,
Make claim and title to the crown of France.
Hugh Capet also, who usurped the crown
Of Charles the Duke of Lorraine, sole heir male
Of the true line and stock of Charles the Great,

37 Pharamond legendary Frankish king   **40 gloze** deceptively explain
away   **45 floods** rivers   **46 Charles the Great** Charlemagne
49 dishonest unchaste   **58 defunction** death   **59 Idly** foolishly
65 which who (as also in l. 67)   **66 heir general** heir through male or
female line

To find his title with some shows of truth,   72
Though, in pure truth, it was corrupt and naught,
Conveyed himself as th' heir to the Lady Lingard,   74
Daughter to Charlemagne, who was the son   75
To Lewis the Emperor, and Lewis the son
Of Charles the Great. Also King Lewis the Tenth,   77
Who was sole heir to the usurper Capet,
Could not keep quiet in his conscience,
Wearing the crown of France, till satisfied
That fair Queen Isabel, his grandmother,
Was lineal of the Lady Ermengard,   82
Daughter to Charles the foresaid Duke of Lorraine;
By the which marriage the line of Charles the Great
Was reunited to the crown of France.
So that, as clear as is the summer's sun,
King Pepin's title and Hugh Capet's claim,
King Lewis his satisfaction, all appear   88
To hold in right and title of the female;
So do the kings of France unto this day.
Howbeit they would hold up this Salic law   91
To bar Your Highness claiming from the female,
And rather choose to hide them in a net   93
Than amply to imbar their crooked titles   94
Usurped from you and your progenitors.

KING
May I with right and conscience make this claim?
CANTERBURY
The sin upon my head, dread sovereign!
For in the Book of Numbers is it writ,   98
When the man dies, let the inheritance   99
Descend unto the daughter. Gracious lord,   100
Stand for your own; unwind your bloody flag!   101

72 find provide   **74 Conveyed himself** passed himself off
75 Charlemagne (Holinshed's and Hall's error, followed by Shakespeare,
for Charles the Bold.)   **77 Lewis the Tenth** (Actually, Louis IX; an error
copied from Holinshed.)   **82 lineal of** descended from   **88 Lewis his
satisfaction** Lewis's conviction   **91 Howbeit** notwithstanding   **93 hide
. . . net** i.e., conceal the weakness of their case in a tangle of contradictions   **94 amply to imbar** frankly to bar claim to   **98 Numbers** (See
Numbers 27:8.)   **99–100 When . . . daughter** (This paraphrase leaves
out an important phrase. Numbers reads, "When a man dies leaving
no son, his patrimony shall pass to his daughter.")   **101 unwind**
unfurl

Look back into your mighty ancestors:
Go, my dread lord, to your great-grandsire's tomb,   103
From whom you claim! Invoke his warlike spirit,
And your great-uncle's, Edward the Black Prince,
Who on the French ground played a tragedy,   106
Making defeat on the full power of France,   107
Whiles his most mighty father on a hill
Stood smiling to behold his lion's whelp   109
Forage in blood of French nobility.   110
O noble English, that could entertain   111
With half their forces the full pride of France
And let another half stand laughing by,
All out of work and cold for action!   114

ELY
Awake remembrance of these valiant dead,
And with your puissant arm renew their feats!
You are their heir; you sit upon their throne;
The blood and courage that renownèd them   118
Runs in your veins; and my thrice-puissant liege
Is in the very May morn of his youth,
Ripe for exploits and mighty enterprises.

EXETER
Your brother kings and monarchs of the earth
Do all expect that you should rouse yourself
As did the former lions of your blood.

WESTMORLAND
They know Your Grace hath cause, and means, and
    might;
So hath Your Highness! Never king of England   126
Had nobles richer and more loyal subjects,
Whose hearts have left their bodies here in England
And lie pavilioned in the fields of France.   129

CANTERBURY
O, let their bodies follow, my dear liege,
With blood, and sword, and fire to win your right!
In aid whereof we of the spiritualty   132

103 **great-grandsire's** i.e., Edward III's 106 **tragedy** i.e., the Battle of Crécy,
1346, a major defeat for the French 107 **power** army 109 **whelp** off-
spring 110 **Forage in** prey on 111 **entertain** engage, encounter 114 **for**
action for want of action 118 **renownèd** brought renown to 126 **So** so
indeed 129 **pavilioned** tented, encamped 132 **spiritualty** clergy

Will raise Your Highness such a mighty sum
As never did the clergy at one time
Bring in to any of your ancestors.

KING
We must not only arm t' invade the French,
But lay down our proportions to defend   137
Against the Scot, who will make road upon us   138
With all advantages.   139

CANTERBURY
They of those marches, gracious sovereign,   140
Shall be a wall sufficient to defend
Our inland from the pilfering borderers.

KING
We do not mean the coursing snatchers only,   143
But fear the main intendment of the Scot,   144
Who hath been still a giddy neighbor to us.   145
For you shall read that my great-grandfather
Never went with his forces into France
But that the Scot on his unfurnished kingdom   148
Came pouring, like the tide into a breach,
With ample and brim fullness of his force,   150
Galling the gleanèd land with hot assays,   151
Girding with grievous siege castles and towns;
That England, being empty of defense,
Hath shook and trembled at th' ill neighborhood.   154

CANTERBURY
She hath been then more feared than harmed, my liege.   155
For hear her but exampled by herself: 156
When all her chivalry hath been in France   157
And she a mourning widow of her nobles,
She hath herself not only well defended

---

137 lay . . . proportions allocate our forces   **138 road** inroad, raid
139 With all advantages whenever a good opportunity presents itself
140 marches borderlands (here, in the north)   **143 coursing snatchers**
mounted raiders   **144 intendment** plan, hostile intent   **145 still**
always.   **giddy** unstable, fickle   **148 unfurnished** unprovided with
defense   **150 brim** absolute, complete   **151 Galling . . . assays** worrying
the land stripped of defenders with hot attacks   **154 neighborhood**
neighborliness   **155 feared** frightened   **156 hear . . . herself** i.e., only
listen how she can be instructed by an example from her own history
157 chivalry knights

But taken and impounded as a stray   160
The King of Scots, whom she did send to France   161
To fill King Edward's fame with prisoner kings
And make her chronicle as rich with praise
As is the ooze and bottom of the sea
With sunken wrack and sumless treasuries.   165

A LORD
But there's a saying very old and true:
     "If that you will France win,
     Then with Scotland first begin."
For once the eagle England being in prey,   169
To her unguarded nest the weasel Scot
Comes sneaking, and so sucks her princely eggs,
Playing the mouse in absence of the cat,
To 'tame and havoc more than she can eat.   173

EXETER
It follows then the cat must stay at home;
Yet that is but a crushed necessity,   175
Since we have locks to safeguard necessaries
And pretty traps to catch the petty thieves.   177
While that the armèd hand doth fight abroad,
Th' advisèd head defends itself at home;   179
For government, though high, and low, and lower,   180
Put into parts, doth keep in one consent,   181
Congreeing in a full and natural close,   182
Like music.

CANTERBURY   Therefore doth heaven divide
The state of man in divers functions,   184
Setting endeavor in continual motion,
To which is fixèd, as an aim or butt,   186
Obedience; for so work the honeybees,
Creatures that by a rule in nature teach

---

160 impounded as a stray (David II of Scotland was captured and
imprisoned in 1346 while Edward III was in France.)   **161 to France**
(Historically, David II was imprisoned in London, not sent to France.)
165 wrack wreckage.   **sumless** inestimable   **169 in prey** absent in
search of prey   **173 'tame** attame, cut into.   **havoc** ravage   **175 crushed
necessity** forced conclusion   **177 pretty** ingenious   **179 advisèd** wise,
prudent   **180 though . . . lower** i.e., though composed of three broad
social ranks   **181 Put into parts** separated into different functions.
one consent mutual harmony   **182 Congreeing** agreeing together.   **close**
musical cadence   **184 divers** various   **186 aim or butt** i.e., target

The act of order to a peopled kingdom.
They have a king, and officers of sorts, 190
Where some, like magistrates, correct at home; 191
Others, like merchants, venture trade abroad;
Others, like soldiers, armèd in their stings,
Make boot upon the summer's velvet buds, 194
Which pillage they with merry march bring home
To the tent royal of their emperor,
Who, busied in his majesty, surveys 197
The singing masons building roofs of gold,
The civil citizens kneading up the honey,
The poor mechanic porters crowding in 200
Their heavy burdens at his narrow gate,
The sad-eyed justice with his surly hum 202
Delivering o'er to executors pale 203
The lazy yawning drone. I this infer,
That many things, having full reference 205
To one consent, may work contrariously. 206
As many arrows loosèd several ways 207
Come to one mark, as many ways meet in one town, 208
As many fresh streams meet in one salt sea,
As many lines close in the dial's center, 210
So may a thousand actions once afoot
End in one purpose, and be all well borne 212
Without defeat. Therefore to France, my liege!
Divide your happy England into four,
Whereof take you one quarter into France,
And you withal shall make all Gallia shake. 216
If we with thrice such powers left at home
Cannot defend our own doors from the dog,
Let us be worried, and our nation lose 219
The name of hardiness and policy. 220

---

190 They . . . king (A common error of early natural history, derived from Aristotle.) **of sorts** of various kinds **191 correct** administer justice **194 Make boot** prey **197 majesty** royal office **200 mechanic** engaged in manual labor **202 sad-eyed** grave-eyed **203 executors** executioners **205–206 having . . . consent** i.e., united by a common understanding **207 loosèd several ways** shot from different directions **208 ways** roads **210 close** come together. **dial's** sundial's **212 borne** carried out, sustained **216 Gallia** France. (Latin name.) **219 worried** torn apart, as by dogs **220 hardiness and policy** bravery and statesmanship

KING
  Call in the messengers sent from the Dauphin.   221
                           [Exeunt some.]
  Now are we well resolved, and by God's help
  And yours, the noble sinews of our power,
  France being ours, we'll bend it to our awe,   224
  Or break it all to pieces. Or there we'll sit,   225
  Ruling in large and ample empery   226
  O'er France and all her almost kingly dukedoms,
  Or lay these bones in an unworthy urn,
  Tombless, with no remembrance over them.
  Either our history shall with full mouth
  Speak freely of our acts, or else our grave,
  Like Turkish mute, shall have a tongueless mouth,
  Not worshiped with a waxen epitaph.   233

    Enter Ambassadors of France.

  Now are we well prepared to know the pleasure
  Of our fair cousin Dauphin; for we hear
  Your greeting is from him, not from the King.
FIRST AMBASSADOR
  May 't please Your Majesty to give us leave
  Freely to render what we have in charge,
  Or shall we sparingly show you far off   239
  The Dauphin's meaning and our embassy?
KING
  We are no tyrant, but a Christian king,
  Unto whose grace our passion is as subject
  As is our wretches fettered in our prisons.
  Therefore with frank and with uncurbèd plainness
  Tell us the Dauphin's mind.
FIRST AMBASSADOR   Thus, then, in few:
  Your Highness, lately sending into France,
  Did claim some certain dukedoms, in the right
  Of your great predecessor, King Edward the Third.
  In answer of which claim, the Prince our master
  Says that you savor too much of your youth,

221 Dauphin heir apparent to the French throne **224 ours** i.e., ours by
right. **our awe** submission to us **225 Or there** either there **226 empery**
dominion **233 Not . . . epitaph** i.e., with not even so much as a wax (as
opposed to bronze) epitaph; one easily effaced **239 sparingly** delicately.
far off i.e., in general terms

And bids you be advised there's naught in France
That can be with a nimble galliard won;   252
You cannot revel into dukedoms there.
He therefore sends you, meeter for your spirit,   254
This tun of treasure, and in lieu of this   255
Desires you let the dukedoms that you claim
Hear no more of you. This the Dauphin speaks.

> [*A casket is presented;*
> *Exeter examines its contents.*]

KING
  What treasure, uncle?
EXETER -   Tennis balls, my liege.
KING
  We are glad the Dauphin is so pleasant with us.
  His present and your pains we thank you for.
  When we have matched our rackets to these balls,
  We will, in France, by God's grace, play a set
  Shall strike his father's crown into the hazard.   263
  Tell him he hath made a match with such a wrangler   264
  That all the courts of France will be disturbed   265
  With chases. And we understand him well,   266
  How he comes o'er us with our wilder days,   267
  Not measuring what use we made of them.
  We never valued this poor seat of England,   269
  And therefore, living hence, did give ourself   270
  To barbarous license—as 'tis ever common
  That men are merriest when they are from home.   272
  But tell the Dauphin I will keep my state,   273
  Be like a king, and show my sail of greatness   274
  When I do rouse me in my throne of France.
  For that I have laid by my majesty   276
  And plodded like a man for working days,   277

---

252 galliard a lively dance   **254 meeter** more fitting   **255 tun** cask
263 crown (1) coin staked in a game (2) symbol of majesty.   **hazard** (1) in tennis of that time, an opening in the wall; hitting the ball into it scored a point (2) jeopardy   **264 wrangler** adversary   **265 courts** (1) tennis courts (2) royal courts   **266 chases** (1) double bounce in tennis, an unsuccessful return (2) pursuits   **267 comes o'er us** taunts me. (*Us* is the royal plural.)   **269 seat** throne   **270 living hence** not frequenting the royal court   **272 from** away from   **273 keep my state** i.e., fulfill the role of king   **274 sail** full swell. (Henry says he has not yet revealed his full majesty in laying claim to France.)   **276 For that** i.e., for my French kingdom.   **277 for** ready for

But I will rise there with so full a glory
That I will dazzle all the eyes of France,
Yea, strike the Dauphin blind to look on us.
And tell the pleasant Prince this mock of his
Hath turned his balls to gunstones, and his soul   282
Shall stand sore chargèd for the wasteful vengeance   283
That shall fly with them; for many a thousand widows
Shall this his mock mock out of their dear husbands,
Mock mothers from their sons, mock castles down,
And some are yet ungotten and unborn   287
That shall have cause to curse the Dauphin's scorn.
But this lies all within the will of God,
To whom I do appeal, and in whose name
Tell you the Dauphin I am coming on
To venge me as I may, and to put forth   292
My rightful hand in a well-hallowed cause.
So get you hence in peace; and tell the Dauphin
His jest will savor but of shallow wit
When thousands weep more than did laugh at it.—
Convey them with safe conduct.—Fare you well.   297

                    Exeunt Ambassadors.
EXETER This was a merry message.
KING
We hope to make the sender blush at it.
Therefore, my lords, omit no happy hour   300
That may give furtherance to our expedition;
For we have now no thought in us but France,
Save those to God, that run before our business.
Therefore let our proportions for these wars   304
Be soon collected, and all things thought upon
That may with reasonable swiftness add
More feathers to our wings; for, God before,   307
We'll chide this Dauphin at his father's door.
Therefore let every man now task his thought,   309
That this fair action may on foot be brought.

                    Flourish. Exeunt.

❖

282 gunstones cannonballs **283 sore chargèd** sorely burdened with
responsibility. **wasteful** destructive **287 yet ungotten** not yet conceived **292 venge** revenge **297 Convey** escort **300 omit . . . hour** lose
no favorable opportunity **304 proportions** levies of men **307 God
before** with God leading, helping **309 task** tax, exercise

2.0 *Enter Chorus.*

CHORUS
  Now all the youth of England are on fire,
  And silken dalliance in the wardrobe lies.   2
  Now thrive the armorers, and honor's thought
  Reigns solely in the breast of every man.
  They sell the pasture now to buy the horse,
  Following the mirror of all Christian kings,
  With wingèd heels, as English Mercurys.   7
  For now sits Expectation in the air,
  And hides a sword from hilts unto the point   9
  With crowns imperial, crowns and coronets,   10
  Promised to Harry and his followers.
  The French, advised by good intelligence   12
  Of this most dreadful preparation,
  Shake in their fear, and with pale policy   14
  Seek to divert the English purposes.
  O England! Model to thy inward greatness,   16
  Like little body with a mighty heart,
  What mightst thou do, that honor would thee do,   18
  Were all thy children kind and natural?
  But see, thy fault France hath in thee found out,
  A nest of hollow bosoms, which he fills
  With treacherous crowns; and three corrupted men,   22
  One, Richard, Earl of Cambridge, and the second,
  Henry, Lord Scroop of Masham, and the third,
  Sir Thomas Grey, knight, of Northumberland,
  Have, for the gilt of France—O guilt indeed!—   26
  Confirmed conspiracy with fearful France,   27
  And by their hands this grace of kings must die,
  If hell and treason hold their promises,
  Ere he take ship for France, and in Southampton.

2.0. Chorus.
2 silken . . . lies i.e., silken apparel and idle pleasure are packed away
7 Mercurys (Mercury, classical messenger of the gods, always wears
winged heels.) **9 hides a sword** i.e., holds up a sword completely
impaled with the prizes of war **10 With . . . coronets** with the crowns
of emperors, kings, and nobles **12 intelligence** espionage **14 pale
policy** fear-inspired intrigue **16 Model to** small replica of **18 would**
would have **22 crowns** coins, money (as a bribe) **26 gilt** gold
27 fearful frightened

Linger your patience on, and we'll digest   31
Th' abuse of distance, force a play.   32
The sum is paid, the traitors are agreed,
The King is set from London, and the scene
Is now transported, gentles, to Southampton.
There is the playhouse now, there must you sit,
And thence to France shall we convey you safe,
And bring you back, charming the narrow seas
To give you gentle pass; for, if we may,   39
We'll not offend one stomach with our play.   40
But, till the King come forth, and not till then,   41
Unto Southampton do we shift our scene.   *Exit.* 42

2.1   *Enter Corporal Nym and Lieutenant Bardolph.*

BARDOLPH   Well met, Corporal Nym.

NYM   Good morrow, Lieutenant Bardolph.

BARDOLPH   What, are Ancient Pistol and you friends   3
yet?

NYM   For my part, I care not. I say little; but when time
shall serve, there shall be smiles—but that shall be as
it may. I dare not fight, but I will wink and hold out   7
mine iron. It is a simple one, but what though? It will   8
toast cheese, and it will endure cold as another man's   9
sword will—and there's an end.   10

BARDOLPH   I will bestow a breakfast to make you
friends, and we'll be all three sworn brothers to
France. Let 't be so, good Corporal Nym.

NYM   Faith, I will live so long as I may, that's the certain

31–32 **digest . . . distance** overcome the difficulties of representing
distance, change of place   **32 force a play** fill out the actions of a play
in spite of difficulties   **39 pass** passage   **40 offend one stomach** (1)
offend anyone's taste in plays (2) make anyone seasick   **41–42 But . . .
scene** i.e., the scene will be shifted to Southampton after a scene in
London. (These lines sound as though added as an afterthought, to
accommodate the inclusion of the comic scene in 2.1.)

2.1. Location: London. A street.
3 Ancient ensign, standard-bearer   **7 wink** shut the eyes   **8 iron**
sword.   **though** of that   **9 endure cold** i.e., doesn't mind being drawn
from its sheath   **10 there's an end** that's all there is to it

of it; and when I cannot live any longer, I will do as I
may. That is my rest; that is the rendezvous of it.   16

BARDOLPH   It is certain, Corporal, that he is married to
Nell Quickly, and certainly she did you wrong, for you
were trothplight to her.   19

NYM   I cannot tell. Things must be as they may. Men
may sleep, and they may have their throats about
them at that time, and some say knives have edges. It
must be as it may. Though Patience be a tired mare,   23
yet she will plod. There must be conclusions. Well, I   24
cannot tell.

Enter Pistol and [Hostess] Quickly.

BARDOLPH   Here comes Ancient Pistol and his wife.
Good Corporal, be patient here.

NYM   How now, mine host Pistol?

PISTOL
Base tike, call'st thou me host?   29
Now, by this hand, I swear, I scorn the term!
Nor shall my Nell keep lodgers.

HOSTESS   No, by my troth, not long; for we cannot lodge
and board a dozen or fourteen gentlewomen that live
honestly by the prick of their needles, but it will be   34
thought we keep a bawdy house straight. [*Nym and
Pistol draw.*] O welladay, Lady! If he be not hewn   36
now, we shall see willful adultery and murder com-   37
mitted.

BARDOLPH   Good Lieutenant! Good Corporal! Offer noth-   39
ing here.   40

NYM   Pish!

PISTOL
Pish for thee, Iceland dog!   42
Thou prick-eared cur of Iceland!

---

16 rest last stake (in the gambling game of primero).   **rendezvous** last
resort   **19 trothplight** betrothed   **23–24 Though . . . plod** i.e., patient
persistence will ultimately achieve its goal. (Nym hints, as he does
elsewhere, at violence toward Pistol.)   **24 conclusions** an end to matters
(i.e., the end must come sometime)   **29 tike** cur   **34 prick** (with a
bawdy double meaning, as also in *Pistol's cock*, l. 53)   **36 welladay**
wellaway, alas.   **Lady** i.e., by Our Lady. (An oath.)   **hewn** struck down
37 adultery (Blunder for *battery?*)   **39–40 Offer nothing** i.e., do not offer
to fight   **42 Iceland dog** a small, shaggy dog often kept as a house pet.
(Pistol's humor is to use extravagant epithets, like this one, tags from
current plays, and scraps of foreign languages.)

HOSTESS Good Corporal Nym, show thy valor, and put   44
  up your sword.   [*They sheathe their swords.*]

NYM Will you shog off? I would have you solus.   46

PISTOL
Solus, egregious dog? O viper vile!
The solus in thy most mervailous face!   48
The solus in thy teeth, and in thy throat,
And in thy hateful lungs, yea, in thy maw, pardie,   50
And, which is worse, within thy nasty mouth!
I do retort the solus in thy bowels;
For I can take, and Pistol's cock is up,   53
And flashing fire will follow.

NYM I am not Barbason; you cannot conjure me. I have   55
  an humor to knock you indifferently well. If you grow
  foul with me, Pistol, I will scour you with my rapier,   57
  as I may, in fair terms. If you would walk off, I would
  prick your guts a little, in good terms, as I may, and
  that's the humor of it.   60

PISTOL
O braggart vile and damnèd furious wight!   61
The grave doth gape, and doting death is near.
Therefore exhale!   [*They draw.*]   63

BARDOLPH Hear me, hear me what I say. He that strikes
  the first stroke, I'll run him up to the hilts, as I am a
  soldier.   [*He draws.*]

PISTOL
An oath of mickle might, and fury shall abate.   67
        [*Pistol and Nym sheathe their swords.*]
[*To Nym*] Give me thy fist, thy forefoot to me give.
Thy spirits are most tall.   69

NYM I will cut thy throat, one time or other, in fair
  terms. That is the humor of it.

PISTOL *Couple a gorge!*   72
  That is the word. I thee defy again.

---

44 valor (She means "calm," "forbearance.") **46 shog off** move
along. **solus** alone **48 mervailous** marvelous **50 maw** belly. **pardie**
i.e., *par Dieu*, by God **53 take** strike **55 Barbason** (Presumably the
name of a fiend. Pistol's preceding speech is a parody of the formula for
exorcising spirits.) **57 foul** (1) foulmouthed (2) fouled from firing and in
need of scouring **60 that's . . . it** that's my mood **61 wight** person
63 exhale draw (sword) **67 mickle** great **69 tall** valiant **72 Couple a
gorge** i.e., *couper la gorge*, cut the throat

O hound of Crete, think'st thou my spouse to get?   74
No, to the spital go,   75
And from the powdering tub of infamy   76
Fetch forth the lazar kite of Cressid's kind,   77
Doll Tearsheet she by name, and her espouse.
I have, and I will hold, the quondam Quickly   79
For the only she; and—*pauca!* There's enough.   80
Go to.

    Enter the Boy.

BOY Mine host Pistol, you must come to my master,
and you, hostess. He is very sick and would to bed.
Good Bardolph, put thy face between his sheets and   84
do the office of a warming pan. Faith, he's very ill.
BARDOLPH Away, you rogue!
HOSTESS By my troth, he'll yield the crow a pudding   87
one of these days. The King has killed his heart. Good   88
husband, come home presently.   *Exit [with Boy].*   89
BARDOLPH Come, shall I make you two friends? We
must to France together. Why the devil should we
keep knives to cut one another's throats?
PISTOL
Let floods o'erswell, and fiends for food howl on!
NYM You'll pay me the eight shillings I won of you at
betting?
PISTOL Base is the slave that pays.
NYM That now I will have. That's the humor of it.
PISTOL As manhood shall compound. Push home.   98
                                [They] draw.
BARDOLPH [*Drawing*] By this sword, he that makes the
first thrust, I'll kill him! By this sword, I will.

---

74 hound of Crete (Parallel to *Iceland dog*, l. 42.)   **75 spital** hospital
76 powdering tub (Originally a tub used for salting beef; here, alluding
to a method of curing venereal disease by sweating.)   **77 lazar . . . kind**
i.e., diseased, leprous whore (a *kite* is a bird of prey) like Cressida, the
fallen woman, who, in Robert Henryson's *Testament of Cresseid*, is
shown as being rejected by Diomede and infected with leprosy
79 quondam former   **80 only she** i.e., only woman in the world.   **pauca**
i.e., in brief   **84 face** (Bardolph's face is fiery with drinking.)
87 yield . . . pudding i.e., be hanged on the gallows and eaten by carrion
birds   **88 his** i.e., Falstaff's   **89 presently** immediately   **98 As . . .
compound** as valor shall settle the matter (in fight)

PISTOL
Sword is an oath, and oaths must have their course.   101
                          [*He sheathes his sword.*]
BARDOLPH Corporal Nym, an thou wilt be friends, be   102
friends; an thou wilt not, why, then, be enemies with
me too. Prithee, put up.   104
NYM I shall have my eight shillings I won of you at
betting?
PISTOL
A noble shalt thou have, and present pay;   107
And liquor likewise will I give to thee,
And friendship shall combine, and brotherhood.
I'll live by Nym, and Nym shall live by me.   110
Is not this just? For I shall sutler be   111
Unto the camp, and profits will accrue.
Give me thy hand.   [*Nym sheathes his sword.*]
NYM I shall have my noble?
PISTOL In cash most justly paid.
NYM Well, then, that's the humor of 't.

          Enter Hostess.

HOSTESS As ever you come of women, come in quickly   117
to Sir John. Ah, poor heart, he is so shaked of a burning quotidian tertian that it is most lamentable to be-   119
hold. Sweet men, come to him.   [*Exit.*]
NYM The King hath run bad humors on the knight,   121
that's the even of it.   122
PISTOL
Nym, thou hast spoke the right.
His heart is fracted and corroborate.   124
NYM The King is a good king, but it must be as it may;
he passes some humors and careers.   126

---

101 Sword is an oath (Quibbling on *sword* as *'s word*, i.e., "God's
word.") **102 an** if **104 put up** i.e., put up your sword **107 noble . . .
pay** i.e., I'll settle for paying you 6 shillings 8 pence ready money
110 Nym (Quibbles on *nim*, meaning "thief.") **111 sutler** seller of
liquor and provisions to the soldiers **117 come of** were born of
119 quotidian tertian (A *quotidian* fever was one that came daily; a
tertian fever, one that came on alternate days, though some authorities
believed that different fevers might mix and intensify their effects.)
121 run bad humors i.e., vented his displeasure **122 even** level truth
124 fracted broken. **corroborate** (Blunder for *broken to pieces* or
corrupted? The word means "strengthened, confirmed.") **126 passes**
lets pass. **careers** gallops, capers

PISTOL
  Let us condole the knight, for, lambkins, we will live.   127
                                      [*Exeunt.*]

                          ❧

2.2   *Enter Exeter, Bedford, and Westmorland.*

BEDFORD
  'Fore God, His Grace is bold to trust these traitors.
EXETER
  They shall be apprehended by and by.
WESTMORLAND
  How smooth and even they do bear themselves!   3
  As if allegiance in their bosoms sat,
  Crownèd with faith and constant loyalty.
BEDFORD
  The King hath note of all that they intend,
  By interception which they dream not of.
EXETER
  Nay, but the man that was his bedfellow,   8
  Whom he hath dulled and cloyed with gracious favors—   9
  That he should, for a foreign purse, so sell
  His sovereign's life to death and treachery!

       Sound trumpets. Enter the King, Scroop,
       Cambridge, and Grey, [and attendants].

KING
  Now sits the wind fair, and we will aboard.   12
  My lord of Cambridge, and my kind lord of Masham,
  And you, my gentle knight, give me your thoughts.
  Think you not that the powers we bear with us   15
  Will cut their passage through the force of France,
  Doing the execution and the act
  For which we have in head assembled them?   18

---

127 condole express our commiseration of or sympathy with.   **lamb-kins** (A term of endearment.)

2.2. Location: Southampton, a seaport on England's southern coast.
3 smooth and even pleasant and calm   **8 bedfellow** i.e., constant compan-ion. (Refers to Scroop.)   **9 dulled** tired   **12 sits . . . fair** the wind blows from a favorable quarter   **15 powers** armed forces   **18 in head** as an army

SCROOP
No doubt, my liege, if each man do his best.
KING
I doubt not that, since we are well persuaded
We carry not a heart with us from hence
That grows not in a fair consent with ours,   22
Nor leave not one behind that doth not wish
Success and conquest to attend on us.
CAMBRIDGE
Never was monarch better feared and loved
Than is Your Majesty. There's not, I think, a subject
That sits in heart-grief and uneasiness
Under the sweet shade of your government.
GREY
True. Those that were your father's enemies
Have steeped their galls in honey, and do serve you   30
With hearts create of duty and of zeal.   31
KING
We therefore have great cause of thankfulness,
And shall forget the office of our hand   33
Sooner than quittance of desert and merit   34
According to the weight and worthiness.
SCROOP
So service shall with steelèd sinews toil,
And labor shall refresh itself with hope,
To do Your Grace incessant services.
KING
We judge no less. Uncle of Exeter,
Enlarge the man committed yesterday   40
That railed against our person. We consider
It was excess of wine that set him on,
And on his more advice we pardon him.   43
SCROOP
That's mercy, but too much security.   44
Let him be punished, sovereign, lest example
Breed, by his sufferance, more of such a kind.   46
KING   O, let us yet be merciful.

---

22 grows . . . consent does not act in harmony   **30 galls** i.e., resentment   **31 create** composed   **33 office** use, function   **34 quittance**
requital   **40 Enlarge** set free   **43 more advice** thinking better of it
44 security overconfidence   **46 sufferance** being pardoned

CAMBRIDGE
  So may Your Highness, and yet punish too.
GREY Sir,
  You show great mercy if you give him life
  After the taste of much correction.   51
KING
  Alas, your too much love and care of me
  Are heavy orisons 'gainst this poor wretch!   53
  If little faults proceeding on distemper   54
  Shall not be winked at, how shall we stretch our eye   55
  When capital crimes, chewed, swallowed, and digested, 56
  Appear before us? We'll yet enlarge that man,   57
  Though Cambridge, Scroop, and Grey, in their dear care
  And tender preservation of our person,
  Would have him punished. And now to our French
    causes.
  Who are the late commissioners?   61
CAMBRIDGE   I one, my lord.
  Your Highness bade me ask for it today.   63
SCROOP So did you me, my liege.
GREY And I, my royal sovereign.
KING [Giving them papers]
  Then, Richard Earl of Cambridge, there is yours;
  There yours, Lord Scroop of Masham; and sir knight,
  Grey of Northumberland, this same is yours.
  Read them, and know I know your worthiness.
  My lord of Westmorland, and uncle Exeter,
  We will aboard tonight.—Why, how now, gentlemen?
  What see you in those papers, that you lose
  So much complexion?—Look ye how they change!   73
  Their cheeks are paper.—Why, what read you there   74
  That have so cowarded and chased your blood
  Out of appearance?
CAMBRIDGE   I do confess my fault,   76
  And do submit me to Your Highness' mercy.

51 **correction** punishment   53 **heavy orisons** weighty prayers, pleas
54 **proceeding on distemper** resulting from excessive drinking   55 **stretch**
open wide, not wink   56 **capital** punishable by death.   **chewed . . . digested** i.e., premeditated   57 **yet** in spite of what you say   61 **late** re-
cently appointed (to serve while Henry is in France)   63 **it** i.e., my
commission   73 **complexion** color   74 **paper** i.e., white as paper
76 **appearance** sight. (Presumably the traitors kneel at this point.)

GREY, SCROOP   To which we all appeal.

KING

The mercy that was quick in us but late   79
By your own counsel is suppressed and killed.
You must not dare, for shame, to talk of mercy,
For your own reasons turn into your bosoms,
As dogs upon their masters, worrying you.   83
See you, my princes and my noble peers,
These English monsters! My lord of Cambridge here,
You know how apt our love was to accord   86
To furnish him with all appurtenants   87
Belonging to his honor; and this man
Hath for a few light crowns lightly conspired   89
And sworn unto the practices of France   90
To kill us here in Hampton. To the which
This knight, no less for bounty bound to us   92
Than Cambridge is, hath likewise sworn. But, O,
What shall I say to thee, Lord Scroop, thou cruel,
Ingrateful, savage, and inhuman creature?
Thou that didst bear the key of all my counsels,
That knew'st the very bottom of my soul,
That almost mightst have coined me into gold,
Wouldst thou have practiced on me for thy use?   99
May it be possible that foreign hire
Could out of thee extract one spark of evil
That might annoy my finger? 'Tis so strange   102
That though the truth of it stands off as gross   103
As black and white, my eye will scarcely see it.
Treason and murder ever kept together,
As two yoke-devils sworn to either's purpose,   106
Working so grossly in a natural cause   107
That admiration did not whoop at them.   108
But thou, 'gainst all proportion, didst bring in   109

79 **quick** alive   83 **worrying** tearing   86 **accord** consent
87 **appurtenants** appurtenances, accessories   89 **light** insignificant.
lightly readily   90 **practices** plots   92 **This knight** i.e., Grey
99 **practiced on** plotted against.   **use** profit (with play on the meaning
"interest derived from usury"; Scroop had served as Lord Treasurer)
102 **annoy** injure   103 **stands . . . gross** appears as obvious   106 **yoke-
devils** partners in a diabolical cause   107–108 **Working . . . them** working together with such obvious fitness, and toward a purpose that
suits them so naturally, that they provoked no outcry of wonder
109 **proportion** fitness of things

Wonder to wait on treason and on murder;   110
And whatsoever cunning fiend it was
That wrought upon thee so preposterously   112
Hath got the voice in hell for excellence.   113
All other devils that suggest by treasons   114
Do botch and bungle up damnation   115
With patches, colors, and with forms being fetched   116
From glistering semblances of piety;   117
But he that tempered thee bade thee stand up,   118
Gave thee no instance why thou shouldst do treason,   119
Unless to dub thee with the name of traitor.
If that same demon that hath gulled thee thus
Should with his lion gait walk the whole world,   122
He might return to vasty Tartar back   123
And tell the legions, "I can never win
A soul so easy as that Englishman's."
O, how hast thou with jealousy infected   126
The sweetness of affiance! Show men dutiful?   127
Why, so didst thou. Seem they grave and learnèd?
Why, so didst thou. Come they of noble family?
Why, so didst thou. Seem they religious?
Why, so didst thou. Or are they spare in diet,   131
Free from gross passion or of mirth or anger,   132
Constant in spirit, not swerving with the blood,   133
Garnished and decked in modest complement,   134
Not working with the eye without the ear,   135
And but in purgèd judgment trusting neither?   136
Such and so finely bolted didst thou seem.   137
And thus thy fall hath left a kind of blot

110 Wonder astonishment (that Scroop should be a murderer).   **wait on**
attend, accompany   **112 wrought** worked.   **preposterously** unnatu-
rally   **113 voice** vote   **114 suggest** tempt   **115–117 Do . . . piety** i.e.,
clumsily conceal their damnable temptation by tricking it out in
attractive-looking semblances of virtue   **118 tempered** directed (to
evil).   **bade** ordered.   **stand up** volunteer   **119 instance** reason
122 lion gait (The devil, according to 1 Peter 5:8, strides about the
world like a roaring lion, "seeking whom he may devour.")   **123 vasty**
vast.   **Tartar** Tartarus, the hell of classical mythology   **126 jealousy**
suspicion   **127 affiance** trust.   **Show** appear   **131 spare** sparing,
frugal   **132 or of** either of   **133 swerving with the blood** sinning
through passion   **134 decked . . . complement** wearing the look of
modesty   **135 Not . . . ear** i.e., trusting neither eye nor ear alone
136 but . . . judgment except on the basis of impartial judgment
137 bolted sifted, refined

To mark the full-fraught man and best endued   139
With some suspicion. I will weep for thee;
For this revolt of thine, methinks, is like
Another fall of man.—Their faults are open.   142
Arrest them to the answer of the law;
And God acquit them of their practices!   144

EXETER I arrest thee of high treason, by the name of
    Richard Earl of Cambridge.
  I arrest thee of high treason, by the name of Henry Lord
    Scroop of Masham.
  I arrest thee of high treason, by the name of Thomas
    Grey, knight, of Northumberland.

SCROOP
Our purposes God justly hath discovered,   151
And I repent my fault more than my death,
Which I beseech Your Highness to forgive,
Although my body pay the price of it.

CAMBRIDGE
For me, the gold of France did not seduce,
Although I did admit it as a motive   156
The sooner to effect what I intended   157
But God be thankèd for prevention,
Which I in sufferance heartily will rejoice,   159
Beseeching God and you to pardon me.

GREY
Never did faithful subject more rejoice
At the discovery of most dangerous treason
Than I do at this hour joy o'er myself,
Prevented from a damnèd enterprise.
My fault, but not my body, pardon, sovereign.

KING
God quit you in his mercy! Hear your sentence.   166
You have conspired against our royal person,
Joined with an enemy proclaimed, and from his coffers

---

139 full-fraught richly laden (with excellent qualities). **endued** endowed **142 open** apparent, obvious **144 practices** plots
151 discovered revealed **156 did . . . motive** i.e., accepted money from France as a means **157 The . . . intended** (Cambridge's real motive, barely hinted at here, was to assist his brother-in-law Edmund Mortimer, fifth Earl of March, to the throne as the standard-bearer of the Yorkist claim against the Lancastrian Henry.) **159 sufferance** my suffering and patient endurance **166 quit** pardon

Received the golden earnest of our death;   169
Wherein you would have sold your king to slaughter,
His princes and his peers to servitude,
His subjects to oppression and contempt,
And his whole kingdom into desolation.
Touching our person seek we no revenge,
But we our kingdom's safety must so tender,   175
Whose ruin you have sought, that to her laws
We do deliver you. Get you therefore hence,
Poor miserable wretches, to your death,
The taste whereof God of his mercy give
You patience to endure, and true repentance
Of all your dear offenses!—Bear them hence.   181

> *Exeunt* [*Cambridge, Scroop,*
>   *and Grey, guarded*].

Now, lords, for France, the enterprise whereof
Shall be to you, as us, like glorious.   183
We doubt not of a fair and lucky war,
Since God so graciously hath brought to light
This dangerous treason lurking in our way
To hinder our beginnings. We doubt not now
But every rub is smoothèd on our way.   188
Then forth, dear countrymen! Let us deliver
Our puissance into the hand of God,   190
Putting it straight in expedition.   191
Cheerly to sea! The signs of war advance!   192
No king of England, if not king of France!

> *Flourish*. [*Exeunt*.]

❖

2.3   *Enter Pistol, Nym, Bardolph, Boy, and Hostess.*

HOSTESS   Prithee, honey-sweet husband, let me bring
thee to Staines.   2

---

169 golden earnest advance payment   **175 tender** regard, hold dear
181 dear grievous   **183 like** alike, equally   **188 But** but that.   **rub**
obstacle. (A bowling term.)   **190 puissance** army   **191 straight in**
expedition immediately in action   **192 signs** ensigns, banners

2.3. London. A street.
2 Staines town on the road from London to Southampton

PISTOL   No; for my manly heart doth earn. Bardolph, be ₃
blithe; Nym, rouse thy vaunting veins; Boy, bristle thy
courage up; for Falstaff he is dead, and we must earn ₅
therefore.

BARDOLPH   Would I were with him, wheresoe'er he
is, either in heaven or in hell!

HOSTESS   Nay, sure he's not in hell. He's in Arthur's ₉
bosom, if ever man went to Arthur's bosom. 'A made ₁₀
a finer end, and went away an it had been any chris- ₁₁
tom child. 'A parted ev'n just between twelve and ₁₂
one, ev'n at the turning o' the tide. For after I saw him
fumble with the sheets, and play with flowers, and
smile upon his finger's end, I knew there was but one
way; for his nose was as sharp as a pen, and 'a babbled ₁₆
of green fields. "How now, Sir John?" quoth I. "What, ₁₇
man? Be o' good cheer." So 'a cried out, "God, God,
God!" three or four times. Now I, to comfort him, bid
him 'a should not think of God; I hoped there was no
need to trouble himself with any such thoughts yet.
So 'a bade me lay more clothes on his feet. I put my
hand into the bed and felt them, and they were as cold
as any stone; then I felt to his knees, and so upward
and upward, and all was as cold as any stone.

NYM   They say he cried out of sack.   ₂₆

HOSTESS   Ay, that 'a did.

BARDOLPH   And of women.

HOSTESS   Nay, that 'a did not.

BOY   Yes, that 'a did, and said they were devils incar-
nate.

HOSTESS   'A could never abide carnation; 'twas a color
he never liked.

BOY   'A said once the devil would have him about
women.

HOSTESS   'A did in some sort, indeed, handle women; ₃₆

3, 5 earn (1) grieve (2) find other employment   **9–10 Arthur's bosom**
(Malapropism for *Abraham's bosom;* see Luke 16:22.)   **10 'A he**   **11 an**
as if   **11–12 christom** newly christened   **16–17 'a babbled of green
fields** (This line contains Theobald's famous emendation. The Folio has
and a Table of greene fields. Falstaff would seem to have been reciting
the Twenty-third Psalm.)   **26 of sack** against sack (a Spanish wine)
36 handle discuss (though an unintended literal sense is also comically
present)

but then he was rheumatic, and talked of the Whore of 37
Babylon.

BOY Do you not remember, 'a saw a flea stick upon
Bardolph's nose, and 'a said it was a black soul burning in hell?

BARDOLPH Well, the fuel is gone that maintained that 42
fire. That's all the riches I got in his service.

NYM Shall we shog? The King will be gone from South- 44
ampton.

PISTOL
Come, let's away. My love, give me thy lips.

　　　　　　　　　　　　　　　[*They kiss.*]

Look to my chattels and my movables.　　　　　　 47

Let senses rule. The word is "Pitch and pay."　　　 48

Trust none,

For oaths are straws, men's faiths are wafer cakes, 　 50

And Holdfast is the only dog, my duck.　　　　　 51

Therefore, *caveto* be thy counselor.　　　　　　 52

Go, clear thy crystals. Yokefellows in arms,　　　 53

Let us to France, like horseleeches, my boys,

To suck, to suck, the very blood to suck!

BOY And that's but unwholesome food, they say.

PISTOL Touch her soft mouth, and march.

BARDOLPH Farewell, hostess.　　　　[*Kissing her.*]

NYM I cannot kiss, that is the humor of it; but adieu.

PISTOL
Let huswifery appear. Keep close, I thee command. 60

HOSTESS Farewell! Adieu!　　　　*Exeunt [separately].*

❖

37 **rheumatic** i.e., feverish, or perhaps an error for *lunatic*. (Pronounced
"rome-atic," preparing for the allusion to the Whore of Babylon, i.e.,
the Church of Rome. See also Revelation 17:4–5.)　42 **fuel** i.e., liquor,
supplied by Falstaff, that has given Bardolph his red face　44 **shog** be
off　47 **chattels . . . movables** personal property　48 **Let . . . pay** i.e.,
keep your eyes and ears open, and let your motto as hostess be "cash
down"　50 **wafer cakes** i.e., easily broken　51 **Holdfast** clamp, staple.
(Compare the proverb "Brag is a good dog, but Holdfast is a better.")
52 **caveto** be cautious. (From the Latin imperative of *caveo*.)　53 **clear
thy crystals** wipe your eyes.　**Yokefellows** i.e., companions　60 **Let . . .
close** i.e., be a thrifty housekeeper, and stay at home

2.4   *Flourish. Enter the French King, the Dauphin,*
       the Dukes of Berri and Brittany, [the Constable,
       and others].

FRENCH KING
  Thus comes the English with full power upon us,
  And more than carefully it us concerns
  To answer royally in our defenses.
  Therefore the Dukes of Berri and of Brittany,
  Of Brabant and of Orleans, shall make forth,
  And you, Prince Dauphin, with all swift dispatch,
  To line and new-repair our towns of war   7
  With men of courage and with means defendant;   8
  For England his approaches makes as fierce
  As waters to the sucking of a gulf.   10
  It fits us then to be as provident
  As fear may teach us, out of late examples   12
  Left by the fatal and neglected English   13
  Upon our fields.
DAUPHIN   My most redoubted Father,   14
  It is most meet we arm us 'gainst the foe;   15
  For peace itself should not so dull a kingdom,
  Though war nor no known quarrel were in question,
  But that defenses, musters, preparations,
  Should be maintained, assembled, and collected
  As were a war in expectation.   20
  Therefore, I say 'tis meet we all go forth
  To view the sick and feeble parts of France.
  And let us do it with no show of fear—
  No, with no more than if we heard that England
  Were busied with a Whitsun morris dance.   25
  For, my good liege, she is so idly kinged,   26
  Her scepter so fantastically borne
  By a vain, giddy, shallow, humorous youth,   28
  That fear attends her not.

2.4. Location: France. The royal court.
7 line reinforce   **8 defendant** defensive   **10 gulf** whirlpool   **12 late**
recent   **13 fatal and neglected** fatally underestimated   **14 redoubted**
respected   **15 meet** appropriate   **20 As were** as if there were
25 Whitsun morris dance folk dance often performed during Whitsun-
tide, in early summer, by persons in fancy costumes and decked with
bells   **26 idly** frivolously   **28 humorous** capricious

CONSTABLE   O, peace, Prince Dauphin!
You are too much mistaken in this king.
Question Your Grace the late ambassadors,
With what great state he heard their embassy,   32
How well supplied with noble counselors,
How modest in exception, and withal   34
How terrible in constant resolution,   35
And you shall find his vanities forespent   36
Were but the outside of the Roman Brutus,   37
Covering discretion with a coat of folly,
As gardeners do with ordure hide those roots   39
That shall first spring and be most delicate.

DAUPHIN
Well, 'tis not so, my Lord High Constable;
But though we think it so, it is no matter.
In cases of defense 'tis best to weigh
The enemy more mighty than he seems.
So the proportions of defense are filled,   45
Which of a weak and niggardly projection   46
Doth, like a miser, spoil his coat with scanting
A little cloth.

FRENCH KING   Think we King Harry strong;
And, princes, look you strongly arm to meet him.   49
The kindred of him hath been fleshed upon us;   50
And he is bred out of that bloody strain
That haunted us in our familiar paths.
Witness our too-much-memorable shame
When Crécy battle fatally was struck,   54
And all our princes captived by the hand
Of that black name, Edward, Black Prince of Wales;
Whiles that his mountain sire, on mountain standing,   57

---

32 state dignity   **34 exception** making objections.   **withal** in addition
35 terrible awesome, terrifying   **36 vanities forespent** follies now a
thing of the past   **37 Brutus** i.e., the elder Brutus, Lucius Junius Brutus, who pretended to be stupid (*brutus*) as a ruse to allay the suspicions of the tyrant Tarquin until the time for overthrow was ripe
39 ordure manure   **45 So . . . filled** i.e., thus an adequate and full
defense is provided   **46 Which . . . projection** i.e., which defense, if it
should be provided on a small and miserly scale   **49 look** be sure
50 kindred i.e., his great-grandfather Edward III and great-uncle
Edward the Black Prince.   **fleshed** initiated in the shedding of blood,
with foretaste of further success   **54 Crécy** French defeat in 1346.
struck waged   **57 mountain sire** i.e., Edward III, born in mountainous
Wales, and of sturdy proportions

Up in the air, crowned with the golden sun,
Saw his heroical seed and smiled to see him   59
Mangle the work of nature and deface
The patterns that by God and by French fathers
Had twenty years been made. This is a stem   62
Of that victorious stock; and let us fear
The native mightiness and fate of him.   64

          Enter a Messenger.

MESSENGER
Ambassadors from Harry King of England
Do crave admittance to Your Majesty.
FRENCH KING
We'll give them present audience. Go and bring them.
          [*Exit Messenger.*]
You see this chase is hotly followed, friends.
DAUPHIN
Turn head and stop pursuit; for coward dogs   69
Most spend their mouths when what they seem to
     threaten   70
Runs far before them. Good my sovereign,
Take up the English short, and let them know   72
Of what a monarchy you are the head.
Self-love, my liege, is not so vile a sin
As self-neglecting.

          Enter Exeter [and other lords].

FRENCH KING   From our brother of England?
EXETER
From him, and thus he greets Your Majesty:
He wills you, in the name of God Almighty,
That you divest yourself and lay apart   78
The borrowed glories that by gift of heaven,
By law of nature and of nations, 'longs   80
To him and to his heirs, namely, the crown
And all wide-stretchèd honors that pertain   82

59 seed i.e., son   **62 twenty years** (i.e., because the warriors thus mangled were born twenty years or so before)   **64 fate** what he is destined
to do   **69 Turn head** stand at bay. (A hunting term.)   **stop pursuit** i.e.,
put an end to their pursuit   **70 Most . . . mouths** bay the loudest
72 Take . . . short quickly dispose of the English   **78 apart** aside
80 'longs belongs   **82 wide-stretchèd** accompanying, reaching over a
broad span

By custom and the ordinance of times   83
Unto the crown of France. That you may know
'Tis no sinister nor no awkward claim,   85
Picked from the wormholes of long-vanished days,
Nor from the dust of old oblivion raked,
He sends you this most memorable line,   88
                              [*Giving a paper*]
In every branch truly demonstrative,
Willing you overlook this pedigree.   90
And when you find him evenly derived   91
From his most famed of famous ancestors,
Edward the Third, he bids you then resign
Your crown and kingdom, indirectly held   94
From him the native and true challenger.   95

FRENCH KING   Or else what follows?

EXETER

Bloody constraint; for if you hide the crown   97
Even in your hearts, there will he rake for it.
Therefore in fierce tempest is he coming,
In thunder and in earthquake, like a Jove,
That if requiring fail, he will compel;   101
And bids you, in the bowels of the Lord,   102
Deliver up the crown, and to take mercy
On the poor souls for whom this hungry war
Opens his vasty jaws; and on your head
Turning the widows' tears, the orphans' cries,
The dead men's blood, the privy maidens' groans,   107
For husbands, fathers, and betrothèd lovers
That shall be swallowed in this controversy.
This is his claim, his threatening, and my message—
Unless the Dauphin be in presence here,
To whom expressly I bring greeting too.

FRENCH KING

For us, we will consider of this further.
Tomorrow shall you bear our full intent
Back to our brother of England.

---

83 ordinance of times decrees of tradition   **85 sinister** illegitimate
88 line pedigree   **90 Willing you overlook** desiring that you look over
91 evenly directly   **94 indirectly** wrongfully   **95 challenger** claimant
97 constraint coercion, compulsion   **101 requiring** requesting
102 bowels mercy, or innermost being. (Cf. Philippians 1:8.)   **107 privy
maidens' groans** maidens' secret grievings

DAUPHIN   For the Dauphin,
  I stand here for him. What to him from England?
EXETER
  Scorn and defiance, slight regard, contempt,
  And anything that may not misbecome   118
  The mighty sender, doth he prize you at.   119
  Thus says my king: an if your father's Highness   120
  Do not, in grant of all demands at large,   121
  Sweeten the bitter mock you sent His Majesty,
  He'll call you to so hot an answer of it   123
  That caves and womby vaultages of France   124
  Shall chide your trespass and return your mock
  In second accent of his ordinance.   126
DAUPHIN
  Say, if my father render fair return,   127
  It is against my will; for I desire
  Nothing but odds with England. To that end,   129
  As matching to his youth and vanity,
  I did present him with the Paris balls.   131
EXETER
  He'll make your Paris Louvre shake for it,   132
  Were it the mistress court of mighty Europe.
  And be assured, you'll find a difference,
  As we his subjects have in wonder found,
  Between the promise of his greener days   136
  And these he masters now. Now he weighs time
  Even to the utmost grain. That you shall read   138
  In your own losses, if he stay in France.
FRENCH KING
  Tomorrow shall you know our mind at full.   140
                                        Flourish.
EXETER
  Dispatch us with all speed, lest that our king

---

118 misbecome be inappropriate for   **119 prize** value, appraise   **120 an
if** if   **121 in grant of** in assenting to.   **at large** in full   **123 of it** for it
124 womby vaultages deep caverns   **126 second accent** echo.   **ordinance**
ordnance, cannon   **127 fair return** courteous reply   **129 odds** strife
131 Paris balls tennis balls   **132 Louvre** the French royal palace
136 greener younger   **138 That . . . read** i.e., you will see this new seri-
ousness manifested   **140 s.d. Flourish** (This trumpet call is sounded as
the French King arises from his throne, thereby dismissing the embassy,
but Exeter boldly insists on speaking further.)

Come here himself to question our delay;
For he is footed in this land already.

FRENCH KING
You shall be soon dispatched with fair conditions.
A night is but small breath and little pause
To answer matters of this consequence.

Flourish. Exeunt.

✤

3.0   *Enter Chorus.*

CHORUS
Thus with imagined wing our swift scene flies   1
In motion of no less celerity   2
Than that of thought. Suppose that you have seen
The well-appointed King at Dover pier   4
Embark his royalty, and his brave fleet   5
With silken streamers the young Phoebus fanning.   6
Play with your fancies, and in them behold
Upon the hempen tackle shipboys climbing;
Hear the shrill whistle, which doth order give
To sounds confused; behold the threaden sails,   10
Borne with th' invisible and creeping wind,
Draw the huge bottoms through the furrowed sea,   12
Breasting the lofty surge. O, do but think   13
You stand upon the rivage and behold   14
A city on th' inconstant billows dancing;
For so appears this fleet majestical,
Holding due course to Harfleur. Follow, follow!
Grapple your minds to sternage of this navy,   18
And leave your England as dead midnight still,
Guarded with grandsires, babies, and old women,
Either past or not arrived to pith and puissance;   21
For who is he whose chin is but enriched
With one appearing hair that will not follow
These culled and choice-drawn cavaliers to France?   24
Work, work your thoughts, and therein see a siege;
Behold the ordnance on their carriages,
With fatal mouths gaping on girded Harfleur.   27
Suppose th' ambassador from the French comes back,
Tells Harry that the King doth offer him
Katharine his daughter, and with her, to dowry,
Some petty and unprofitable dukedoms.

3.0. Chorus.
1 imagined wing wings of imagination   **2 celerity** speed   **4 well-appointed** well-equipped.   **Dover** (Seemingly an error for Hampton, i.e., Southampton.)   **5 brave** handsome   **6 the ... fanning** i.e., fluttering against the rising sun   **10 threaden** woven of thread   **12 bottoms** hulls of ships   **13 surge** swell of the sea   **14 rivage** shore   **18 Grapple** attach, hook.   **to sternage** to the sterns   **21 pith** strength   **24 choice-drawn** carefully selected   **27 fatal** deadly.   **girded** besieged

The offer likes not; and the nimble gunner   32
With linstock now the devilish cannon touches,   33
              Alarum, and chambers go off.
And down goes all before them. Still be kind,
And eke out our performance with your mind.

                          Exit.

3.1   *Enter the King, Exeter, Bedford, and*
       Gloucester. Alarum, [with soldiers carrying]
       scaling ladders at Harfleur.

KING
  Once more unto the breach, dear friends, once more,
  Or close the wall up with our English dead!
  In peace there's nothing so becomes a man
  As modest stillness and humility.
  But when the blast of war blows in our ears,
  Then imitate the action of the tiger:
  Stiffen the sinews, conjure up the blood,
  Disguise fair nature with hard-favored rage.   8
  Then lend the eye a terrible aspect: 9
  Let it pry through the portage of the head   10
  Like the brass cannon; let the brow o'erwhelm it   11
  As fearfully as doth a gallèd rock   12
  O'erhang and jutty his confounded base,   13
  Swilled with the wild and wasteful ocean.   14
  Now set the teeth and stretch the nostril wide,
  Hold hard the breath, and bend up every spirit
  To his full height. On, on, you noblest English,
  Whose blood is fet from fathers of war-proof!   18

---

32 likes pleases   **33 linstock** staff holding a gunner's match   **s.d. Alarum**
call to arms.   **chambers** small cannon (fired off backstage, or "within")

3.1. Location: France. Before Harfleur.
s.d. scaling ladders (Presumably these are set up against the facade of
the tiring house, backstage, which is perceived to be the walls of
Harfleur.)   **8 hard-favored** unsightly, ugly   **9 terrible aspect** terrifying
appearance   **10 portage** portholes, eyes   **11 o'erwhelm** project over
12 fearfully frighteningly.   **gallèd** washed away, undermined   **13 jutty**
overhang.   **his confounded** its ruined   **14 Swilled** washed.   **wasteful**
destructive   **18 fet** fetched, derived.   **of war-proof** proved in war

Fathers that, like so many Alexanders,   19
Have in these parts from morn till even fought,   20
And sheathed their swords for lack of argument.   21
Dishonor not your mothers; now attest
That those whom you called fathers did beget you.
Be copy now to men of grosser blood,   24
And teach them how to war. And you, good yeomen,
Whose limbs were made in England, show us here
The mettle of your pasture. Let us swear   27
That you are worth your breeding, which I doubt not,
For there is none of you so mean and base
That hath not noble luster in your eyes.
I see you stand like greyhounds in the slips,   31
Straining upon the start. The game's afoot!
Follow your spirit, and upon this charge   33
Cry, "God for Harry! England and Saint George!"   34
    Alarum, and chambers go off. [Exeunt.]

3.2   *Enter Nym, Bardolph, Pistol, and Boy.*

BARDOLPH On, on, on, on, on! To the breach, to the
  breach!
NYM Pray thee, Corporal, stay. The knocks are too hot,
  and for mine own part I have not a case of lives. The   4
  humor of it is too hot, that is the very plainsong of it.   5
PISTOL
  "The plainsong" is most just, for humors do abound.
  "Knocks go and come; God's vassals drop and die;
     And sword and shield
     In bloody field
    Doth win immortal fame."

---

19 Alexanders (Alexander grieved that there were no new worlds for him
to conquer.) **20 even** evening **21 argument** i.e., opposition **24 copy**
models **27 mettle . . . pasture** quality of your breeding. (Literally,
pasture means "feeding.") **31 slips** leashes **33 Follow your spirit** i.e.,
obey the impulse of your vital powers (as also in l. 16) **34 Saint George**
patron saint of England

**3.2. Location: Before Harfleur, as in the previous scene; the action is
essentially continuous.**
4 case set **5 plainsong** i.e., simple truth

BOY Would I were in an alehouse in London! I would
give all my fame for a pot of ale and safety.

PISTOL And I:
"If wishes would prevail with me,
My purpose should not fail with me,
    But thither would I hie."   16

BOY
"As duly, but not as truly,
    As bird doth sing on bough."

Enter Fluellen.

FLUELLEN Up to the breach, you dogs! Avaunt, you cul-   19
lions!   [*Driving them forward.*]   20

PISTOL
Be merciful, great duke, to men of mold.   21
Abate thy rage, abate thy manly rage,
Abate thy rage, great duke!
Good bawcock, bate thy rage! Use lenity, sweet chuck!   24

NYM These be good humors! Your honor runs bad hu-   25
mors.   *Exit* [*with all but Boy*].   26

BOY As young as I am, I have observed these three
swashers. I am boy to them all three, but all they three, 28
though they would serve me, could not be man to me;   29
for indeed three such antics do not amount to a man.   30
For Bardolph, he is white-livered and red-faced, by the   31
means whereof 'a faces it out but fights not. For Pistol, 32
he hath a killing tongue and a quiet sword, by the
means whereof 'a breaks words and keeps whole   34
weapons. For Nym, he hath heard that men of few
words are the best men, and therefore he scorns to say
his prayers, lest 'a should be thought a coward; but

16 **hie** hasten 19 **Avaunt** begone 19–20 **cullions** rascals. (Original
meaning: "testicles.") 21 **men of mold** mere mortals 24 **bawcock**
fine fellow. (French *beau coq.*) **chuck** (A term of endearment.)
25–26 **Your . . . humors** i.e., you are behaving very idiosyncratically,
your honor. (Addressed to Fluellen, who is doubtless threatening or
beating them to make them go forward.) 28 **swashers** swashbuck-
lers 29 **man** (1) master (2) a manly, brave person 30 **antics** buffoons,
zanies 31 **For** as for (also in ll. 32 and 35). **white-livered** i.e., cowardly. (In extreme fear the blood was thought to sink below the liver,
leaving it bloodless.) 32 **'a faces it out** i.e., he puts on a brave front
34 **breaks words** (1) misuses language and fails to keep his word (2)
uses words as weapons

his few bad words are matched with as few good
deeds, for 'a never broke any man's head but his own,
and that was against a post when he was drunk. They
will steal anything and call it purchase. Bardolph 41
stole a lute case, bore it twelve leagues, and sold it for
three halfpence. Nym and Bardolph are sworn brothers in filching, and in Calais they stole a fire shovel. I
knew by that piece of service the men would carry 45
coals. They would have me as familiar with men's 46
pockets as their gloves or their handkerchiefs, which
makes much against my manhood, if I should take 48
from another's pocket to put into mine, for it is plain
pocketing up of wrongs. I must leave them and seek 50
some better service. Their villainy goes against my 51
weak stomach, and therefore I must cast it up.   *Exit.* 52

Enter Gower [and Fluellen, meeting].

GOWER   Captain Fluellen, you must come presently to
the mines. The Duke of Gloucester would speak with 54
you.
FLUELLEN   To the mines? Tell you the Duke it is not so
good to come to the mines; for look you, the mines is
not according to the disciplines of the war. The con- 58
cavities of it is not sufficient. For look you, th' athver- 59
sary, you may discuss unto the Duke, look you, is digt 60
himself four yard under the countermines. By Cheshu, 61
I think 'a will plow up all, if there is not better direc- 62
tions.

41 purchase (Thieves' cant for "stolen goods.")   **45–46 carry coals** i.e.,
submit to insult or degradation   **48 makes** i.e., goes   **50 pocketing . . .
wrongs** (1) putting up with insults (2) receiving stolen goods
51–52 goes . . . stomach (1) goes against my inclination (2) makes me
sick   **52 cast it up** (1) cast it aside (2) vomit it   **s.d. Exit** (A scene
break may occur here, though it is not marked as such in most editions.
Possibly Fluellen did not leave the stage at l. 26.)   **54 mines** undermin-
ing operation in a siege   **58 disciplines of the war** science of warfare
(about which there were many books from Greek and Roman times
down to the Renaissance; Fluellen's humor involves an obsession with
this study and a preference for traditional methods)   **58–59 concavities**
i.e., depth   **59–60 athversary** (Fluellen's pronunciation of *adversary*.)
60 discuss explain   **60–61 is digt . . . countermines** has dug himself
countermines four yards beneath our mines   **61 Cheshu** Jesu, Jesus
62 plow blow. (In Fluellen's Welsh dialect, "p" is regularly substituted
for "b" and "f" for "v.")

GOWER The Duke of Gloucester, to whom the order of
the siege is given, is altogether directed by an Irish-
man, a very valiant gentleman, i' faith.

FLUELLEN It is Captain Macmorris, is it not?

GOWER I think it be.

FLUELLEN By Cheshu, he is an ass, as in the world! I
will verify as much in his beard. He has no more di- 70
rections in the true disciplines of the wars, look you,
of the Roman disciplines, than is a puppy dog.

Enter Macmorris and Captain Jamy.

GOWER Here 'a comes, and the Scots captain, Captain
Jamy, with him.

FLUELLEN Captain Jamy is a marvelous falorous gentleman, that is certain, and of great expedition and 76
knowledge in th' aunchient wars, upon my particular
knowledge of his directions. By Cheshu, he will maintain his argument as well as any military man in the
world, in the disciplines of the pristine wars of the 80
Romans.

JAMY I say gud day, Captain Fluellen.

FLUELLEN Good e'en to your worship, good Captain 83
James.

GOWER How now, Captain Macmorris, have you quit
the mines? Have the pioners given o'er? 86

MACMORRIS By Chrish, la, 'tish ill done! The work ish
give over, the trompet sound the retreat. By my hand
I swear, and my father's soul, the work ish ill done; it
ish give over. I would have blowed up the town, so
Chrish save me, la, in an hour. O, 'tish ill done, 'tish ill
done! By my hand, 'tish ill done!

FLUELLEN Captain Macmorris, I beseech you now, will
you voutsafe me, look you, a few disputations with 94
you, as partly touching or concerning the disciplines
of the war, the Roman wars, in the way of argument,
look you, and friendly communication—partly to sat-
isfy my opinion, and partly for the satisfaction, look
you, of my mind, as touching the direction of the military discipline, that is the point.

70 in his beard i.e., to his face **76 expedition** readiness of argument,
quickness of wit **80 pristine** ancient **83 Good e'en** good afternoon or
evening **86 pioners** sappers, diggers **94 voutsafe** vouchsafe, permit

JAMY   It sall be vary gud, gud feith, gud captens bath,   101
and I sall quite you with gud leve, as I may pick occa-   102
sion. That sall I, marry.   103

MACMORRIS   It is no time to discourse, so Chrish save
me! The day is hot, and the weather, and the wars,
and the King, and the dukes. It is no time to discourse.
The town is beseeched, and the trumpet call us to the   107
breach, and we talk, and, be Chrish, do nothing. 'Tis   108
shame for us all. So God sa' me, 'tis shame to stand
still, it is shame, by my hand! And there is throats to
be cut, and works to be done, and there ish nothing
done, so Chrish sa' me, la!   112

JAMY   By the Mess, ere theise eyes of mine take them-   113
selves to slomber, ay'll de gud service, or I'll lig i' the   114
grund for it, ay, or go to death! And I'll pay 't as val-
orously as I may, that sall I suerly do, that is the breff   116
and the long. Marry, I wad full fain heard some ques-   117
tion 'tween you tway.   118

FLUELLEN   Captain Macmorris, I think, look you, under
your correction, there is not many of your nation—

MACMORRIS   Of my nation? What ish my nation? Ish a   121
villain, and a bastard, and a knave, and a rascal? What
ish my nation? Who talks of my nation?

FLUELLEN   Look you, if you take the matter otherwise
than is meant, Captain Macmorris, peradventure I
shall think you do not use me with that affability as in
discretion you ought to use me, look you, being as
good a man as yourself, both in the disciplines of war
and in the derivation of my birth, and in other particu-
larities.

MACMORRIS   I do not know you so good a man as myself. So Chrish save me, I will cut off your head!

GOWER   Gentlemen both, you will mistake each other.   133

---

101 bath both   **102 quite** requite, answer.   **with gud leve** with good
leave, with your kind permission   **103 marry** indeed. (Originally, *by the
Virgin Mary.*)   **107 beseeched** besieged   **108 be** by   **112 Chrish sa' me**
Christ save me   **113 Mess** Mass   **114 ay'll de** I'll do.   **lig** lie   **116 breff**
brief   **117 wad full fain heard** would very willingly have heard
117–118 question discussion   **121 What ish** i.e., what about.   **Ish** i.e.,
(anyone who says anything against my nationality) is   **133 will mistake**
(Two possible meanings: [1] insist on misunderstanding [2] are going to
misunderstand.)

JAMY   Ah, that's a foul fault!   *A parley [is sounded].*   134
GOWER   The town sounds a parley.
FLUELLEN   Captain Macmorris, when there is more better opportunity to be required, look you, I will be so   137
bold as to tell you I know the disciplines of war; and
there is an end.   *Exit [with others].*

3.3   *[Enter the Governor and some citizens on the*
walls.] Enter the King [Henry] and all his train
before the gates.

KING
How yet resolves the Governor of the town?
This is the latest parle we will admit.   2
Therefore to our best mercy give yourselves,
Or, like to men proud of destruction,   4
Defy us to our worst; for as I am a soldier,
A name that in my thoughts becomes me best,
If I begin the battery once again,   7
I will not leave the half-achievèd Harfleur
Till in her ashes she lie burièd.
The gates of mercy shall be all shut up,
And the fleshed soldier, rough and hard of heart,   11
In liberty of bloody hand shall range
With conscience wide as hell, mowing like grass   13
Your fresh fair virgins and your flowering infants.
What is it then to me if impious war,
Arrayed in flames like to the prince of fiends,
Do with his smirched complexion all fell feats   17
Enlinked to waste and desolation?

---

134 s.d. parley trumpet summons to a negotiation   **137 required** found

3.3. Location: Before the gates of Harfleur, as in the previous scene. The
action is essentially continuous, as usually in battle sequences; possibly
some of the captains in 3.2 do not need to exit here. The gates are
represented by the tiring house facade. Those who appear *on the walls*
are seen in the gallery backstage.
2 latest parle last parley   **4 like . . . destruction** i.e., like men elated at the
prospect of death and glorying in destruction   **7 battery** attack
11 fleshed made fierce with the taste of blood   **13 wide as hell** i.e., letting
anything pass   **17 smirched** discolored, covered with grime.   **fell** savage

What is 't to me, when you yourselves are cause,
If your pure maidens fall into the hand
Of hot and forcing violation?
What rein can hold licentious wickedness
When down the hill he holds his fierce career?   23
We may as bootless spend our vain command   24
Upon th' enragèd soldiers in their spoil
As send precepts to the leviathan   26
To come ashore. Therefore, you men of Harfleur,
Take pity of your town and of your people
Whiles yet my soldiers are in my command,
Whiles yet the cool and temperate wind of grace   30
O'erblows the filthy and contagious clouds   31
Of heady murder, spoil, and villainy.   32
If not, why, in a moment look to see   33
The blind and bloody soldier with foul hand   34
Defile the locks of your shrill-shrieking daughters;
Your fathers taken by the silver beards
And their most reverend heads dashed to the walls;
Your naked infants spitted upon pikes,
Whiles the mad mothers with their howls confused
Do break the clouds, as did the wives of Jewry   40
At Herod's bloody-hunting slaughtermen.   41
What say you? Will you yield, and this avoid,
Or, guilty in defense, be thus destroyed?   43

GOVERNOR
Our expectation hath this day an end.
The Dauphin, whom of succors we entreated,   45
Returns us that his powers are yet not ready   46
To raise so great a siege. Therefore, great King,
We yield our town and lives to thy soft mercy.
Enter our gates, dispose of us and ours,
For we no longer are defensible.   50

---

23 he . . . career it makes its fierce gallop **24 bootless** fruitlessly
26 precepts written summons. **leviathan** whale **30 grace** mercy
31 O'erblows blows away. (Contagion was thought to reside in clouds
and mists.) **32 heady** violent; headstrong **33 look** expect **34 blind**
i.e., blinded with lust and rage **40 Jewry** Judaea **41 Herod's . . .
slaughtermen** (For the account of Herod's slaughter of the innocent
children in his attempt to murder the infant Jesus, see Matthew
2:16–18.) **43 in defense** i.e., by not surrendering **45 of succors** for
help **46 Returns** replies to **50 defensible** able to defend ourselves

KING
  Open your gates. [*Exit Governor.*] Come, uncle Exeter,
  Go you and enter Harfleur; there remain,
  And fortify it strongly 'gainst the French.
  Use mercy to them all. For us, dear uncle,   54
  The winter coming on and sickness growing
  Upon our soldiers, we will retire to Calais.
  Tonight in Harfleur will we be your guest;
  Tomorrow for the march are we addressed.   58
                Flourish, and enter the town.

3.4   *Enter Katharine and [Alice,] an old*
       gentlewoman.

KATHARINE   Alice, tu as été en Angleterre, et tu parles 1
  bien le langage.
ALICE   Un peu, madame.
KATHARINE   Je te prie, m'enseignez; il faut que
  j'apprenne à parler. Comment appelez-vous la main
  en anglais?
ALICE   La main? Elle est appelée de hand.
KATHARINE   De hand. Et les doigts?
ALICE   Les doigts? Ma foi, j'oublie les doigts; mais je me
  souviendrai. Les doigts? Je pense qu'ils sont appelés 10
  de fingres; oui, de fingres.
KATHARINE   La main, de hand; les doigts, de fingres.
  Je pense que je suis le bon écolier; j'ai gagné deux

---

54 **For** as for   58 **addressed** prepared

3.4. Location: The French court at Rouen.
Translation:
KATHARINE Alice, you have been in England and speak the language well.
ALICE A little, my lady.
KATHARINE I pray you teach me; I have to learn to speak it. What do you
  call *la main* in English?
ALICE *La main?* It is called de hand.
KATHARINE De hand. And *les doigts?*
ALICE *Les doigts?* Dear me, I forget *les doigts;* but I shall remember. I think
  that they are called de fingres; yes, de fingres.
KATHARINE *La main,* de hand; *les doigts,* de fingres. I think that I am a
  clever scholar; I have learned two English words in no time. What do
  you call *les ongles?*

mots d'anglais vitement. Comment appelez-vous les
ongles?

ALICE Les ongles? Nous les appelons de nailes.

KATHARINE De nailes. Écoutez, dites-moi si je parle
bien: de hand, de fingres, et de nailes.

ALICE C'est bien dit, madame; il est fort bon anglais.

KATHARINE Dites-moi l'anglais pour le bras.   20

ALICE De arm, madame.

KATHARINE Et le coude?

ALICE D' elbow.

KATHARINE D' elbow. Je m'en fais la répétition de tous
les mots que vous m'avez appris dès à présent.

ALICE Il est trop difficile, madame, comme je pense.

KATHARINE Excusez-moi, Alice; écoutez: d' hand, de fingre, de nailes, d' arma, de bilbow.

ALICE D' elbow, madame.

KATHARINE O Seigneur Dieu, je m'en oublie! D' elbow. 30
Comment appelez-vous le col?

ALICE De nick, madame.

KATHARINE De nick. Et le menton?

ALICE De chin.

KATHARINE De sin. Le col, de nick; le menton, de sin.

ALICE Oui. Sauf votre honneur, en vérité, vous pro-
noncez les mots aussi droit que les natifs d'Angleterre.

ALICE *Les ongles?* We call them de nailes.

KATHARINE De nailes. Listen; tell me whether or not I speak correctly: de
hand, de fingres, and de nailes.

ALICE That is correct, my lady; it is very good English.

KATHARINE Tell me the English for *le bras.*

ALICE De arm, my lady.

KATHARINE And *le coude*?

ALICE D' elbow.

KATHARINE D' elbow. I am going to repeat all the words you have taught
me so far.

ALICE It is too hard, my lady, I fear.

KATHARINE Pardon me, Alice; listen: d' hand, de fingre, de nailes, d' arma,
de bilbow.

ALICE D' elbow, my lady.

KATHARINE O Lord, I can't remember! D' elbow. What do you call *le col*?

ALICE De nick, my lady.

KATHARINE De nick. And *le menton*?

ALICE De chin.

KATHARINE De sin. *Le col,* de nick; *le menton,* de sin.

ALICE Yes. If I may say so, really you pronounce the words just as correctly
as native Englishmen.

KATHARINE   Je ne doute point d'apprendre, par la grâce de Dieu, et en peu de temps.

ALICE   N'avez-vous pas déjà oublié ce que je vous ai 40 enseigné?

KATHARINE   Non, je réciterai à vous promptement: d' hand, de fingre, de mailes—

ALICE   De nailes, madame.

KATHARINE   De nailes, de arm, de ilbow.

ALICE   Sauf votre honneur, d' elbow.

KATHARINE   Ainsi dis-je; d' elbow, de nick, et de sin. Comment appelez-vous le pied et la robe?

ALICE   Le foot, madame, et le count.

KATHARINE   Le foot et le count! O Seigneur Dieu! Ils 50 sont les mots de son mauvais, corruptible, gros, et impudique, et non pour les dames d'honneur d'user. Je ne voudrais prononcer ces mots devant les seigneurs de France pour tout le monde. Foh! Le foot et le count! Néanmoins, je réciterai une autre fois ma leçon ensemble: d' hand, de fingre, de nailes, de arm, d' elbow, de nick, de sin, de foot, le count.

ALICE   Excellent, madame!

KATHARINE   C'est assez pour une fois. Allons-nous à dîner.   *Exit [with Alice].* 60

KATHARINE I have no doubt that I shall learn, with God's help, in a very short time.

ALICE Haven't you already forgotten what I have taught you?

KATHARINE No. I shall recite to you at once: d' hand, de fingre, de mailes—

ALICE De nailes, my lady.

KATHARINE De nailes, de arm, de ilbow.

ALICE By your leave, d' elbow.

KATHARINE That's what I said; d' elbow, de nick, and de sin. What do you call *le pied* and *la robe*?

ALICE Le foot, my lady, and le count. [As she pronounces them, *foot* sounds to Katharine like *foutre*, fornicate, and *count* (for *gown*) sounds like French for the female sexual organ, *cunt* in English.]

KATHARINE Le foot and le count! O Lord! Those are naughty words, wicked, coarse, and immodest, and are not fit to be used by ladies. I wouldn't say those words before French gentlemen for the whole world. Bah! Le foot and le count! Nevertheless, I shall recite my whole lesson once more: d' hand, de fingre, de nailes, de arm, d' elbow, de nick, de sin, de foot, le count.

ALICE Excellent, my lady.

KATHARINE That's enough for one time. Let's go to dinner.

3.5   *Enter the King of France, the Dauphin, [the Duke of Brittany,] the Constable of France, and others.*

FRENCH KING
  'Tis certain he hath passed the River Somme.
CONSTABLE
  And if he be not fought withal, my lord,   2
  Let us not live in France; let us quit all
  And give our vineyards to a barbarous people.
DAUPHIN
  O Dieu vivant! Shall a few sprays of us,   5
  The emptying of our fathers' luxury,   6
  Our scions, put in wild and savage stock,   7
  Spirt up so suddenly into the clouds   8
  And overlook their grafters?   9
BRITTANY
  Normans, but bastard Normans, Norman bastards!
  Mort de ma vie, if they march along   11
  Unfought withal, but I will sell my dukedom   12
  To buy a slobbery and a dirty farm   13
  In that nook-shotten isle of Albion.   14
CONSTABLE
  Dieu de batailles, where have they this mettle?   15
  Is not their climate foggy, raw, and dull,
  On whom as in despite the sun looks pale,   17
  Killing their fruit with frowns? Can sodden water,   18
  A drench for sur-reined jades, their barley broth,   19
  Decoct their cold blood to such valiant heat?   20
  And shall our quick blood, spirited with wine,   21
  Seem frosty? O, for honor of our land,

3.5. Location: The French court at Rouen.
2 withal with (as also in l. 12)   5 Dieu vivant living God.   sprays off-shoots, illegitimate stock   6 fathers' luxury ancestors' lust   7 scions grafts.   put in grafted upon   8 Spirt shoot, sprout   9 overlook rise above.   grafters trees from which scions are taken   11 Mort de ma vie death of my life, i.e., may my life end   12 but I will i.e., if I do not   13 slobbery slovenly   14 nook-shotten full of nooks and angles. (Refers to the coastline.)   isle of Albion island of England, Scotland, and Wales   15 Dieu de batailles God of battles.   where from where   17 despite contempt   18 sodden water boiled water   19 drench . . . jades medicinal drink for overridden horses.   barley broth ale   20 Decoct warm up   21 quick lively

Let us not hang like roping icicles   23
Upon our houses' thatch, whiles a more frosty people
Sweat drops of gallant youth in our rich fields!
"Poor" may we call them in their native lords.   26

DAUPHIN   By faith and honor,
Our madams mock at us and plainly say   28
Our mettle is bred out, and they will give   29
Their bodies to the lust of English youth
To new-store France with bastard warriors.   31

BRITTANY
They bid us to the English dancing schools   32
And teach lavoltas high and swift corantos,   33
Saying our grace is only in our heels   34
And that we are most lofty runaways.   35

FRENCH KING
Where is Montjoy the herald? Speed him hence.   36
Let him greet England with our sharp defiance.
Up, princes, and, with spirit of honor edged   38
More sharper than your swords, hie to the field!   39
Charles Delabreth, High Constable of France,
You Dukes of Orleans, Bourbon, and of Berri,
Alençon, Brabant, Bar, and Burgundy,
Jaques Chatillion, Rambures, Vaudemont,
Beaumont, Grandpré, Roussi, and Faulconbridge,
Foix, Lestrelles, Boucicault, and Charolais,
High dukes, great princes, barons, lords, and knights,
For your great seats now quit you of great shames.   47
Bar Harry England, that sweeps through our land   48
With pennons painted in the blood of Harfleur.   49
Rush on his host, as doth the melted snow   50
Upon the valleys, whose low vassal seat

23 **roping** hanging down like a rope   26 **Poor . . . lords** i.e., our fields,
though rich in themselves, may be called poor in that they are owned by
a spiritless aristocracy. (*Them* refers to "our fields"; *in* means "in
respect to.")   28 **madams** wives, ladies   29 **bred out** exhausted by
breeding   31 **new-store** newly supply   32 **bid us** bid us go   33 **lavoltas,
corantos** fashionable dances   34 **in our heels** (1) in dancing gracefully
(2) in running away   35 **lofty** (1) noble (2) leaping.   **runaways** cowards
(but referring also to the movements of the dances)   36 **Montjoy** title of
the chief herald of France   38 **edged** given a sharp edge   39 **hie** hasten   47 **For** in the name of, in defense of.   **seats** positions.   **quit** rid,
free   48 **Bar** stop, bar the way of   49 **pennons** banners, streamers
50 **host** army

The Alps doth spit and void his rheum upon.   52
Go down upon him—you have power enough—
And in a captive chariot into Rouen
Bring him our prisoner.

CONSTABLE   This becomes the great.   55
Sorry am I his numbers are so few,
His soldiers sick and famished in their march,
For I am sure, when he shall see our army,
He'll drop his heart into the sink of fear   59
And for achievement offer us his ransom.   60

FRENCH KING
Therefore, Lord Constable, haste on Montjoy,   61
And let him say to England that we send
To know what willing ransom he will give.
Prince Dauphin, you shall stay with us in Rouen.

DAUPHIN
Not so, I do beseech Your Majesty.

FRENCH KING
Be patient, for you shall remain with us.
Now forth, Lord Constable and princes all,
And quickly bring us word of England's fall.   *Exeunt.*

❖

3.6   *Enter Captains, English and Welsh: Gower and Fluellen, [meeting].*

GOWER   How now, Captain Fluellen? Come you from
the bridge?   2

FLUELLEN   I assure you there is very excellent services   3
committed at the bridge.

GOWER   Is the Duke of Exeter safe?

FLUELLEN   The Duke of Exeter is as magnanimous as
Agamemnon, and a man that I love and honor with   7

---

52 rheum i.e., waters   **55 becomes the great** befits greatness   **59 sink**
pit   **60 for achievement** instead of achieving victory, as his sole accomplishment   **61 haste** prod, hurry

3.6. Location: The English camp in northern France.
2 bridge (According to Holinshed, the French were beaten in their
attempt to break down the bridge over the Ternoise. The audience is not
told this, however, and might assume the river to be the Somme, mentioned in 3.5.1.)   **3 services** exploits (as also in l. 71)   **7 Agamemnon**
leader of the Greeks against Troy

my soul, and my heart, and my duty, and my live, 8
and my living, and my uttermost power. He is not—
God be praised and blessed!—any hurt in the world,
but keeps the bridge most valiantly, with excellent discipline. There is an aunchient lieutenant there at the 12
pridge, I think in my very conscience he is as valiant
a man as Mark Antony, and he is a man of no esti- 14
mation in the world, but I did see him do as gallant 15
service.

GOWER   What do you call him?

FLUELLEN   He is called Aunchient Pistol.

GOWER   I know him not.

    Enter Pistol.

FLUELLEN   Here is the man.

PISTOL

  Captain, I thee beseech to do me favors.
  The Duke of Exeter doth love thee well.

FLUELLEN   Ay, I praise God, and I have merited some
  love at his hands.

PISTOL

  Bardolph, a soldier, firm and sound of heart,
  And of buxom valor, hath, by cruel fate   26
  And giddy Fortune's furious fickle wheel,
  That goddess blind
  That stands upon the rolling restless stone—

FLUELLEN   By your patience, Aunchient Pistol. Fortune
is painted blind, with a muffler afore her eyes, to sig- 31
nify to you that Fortune is blind; and she is painted
also with a wheel, to signify to you, which is the moral
of it, that she is turning, and inconstant, and mutabil-
ity, and variation; and her foot, look you, is fixed upon
a spherical stone, which rolls, and rolls, and rolls. In
good truth, the poet is make a most excellent descrip- 37
tion of it. Fortune is an excellent moral.   38

PISTOL

  Fortune is Bardolph's foe, and frowns on him;   39

---

8 live life   **12 aunchient lieutenant** (Pistol is elsewhere given the rank of
ancient, or ensign.)   **14–15 estimation** fame   **26 buxom** (1) vigorous (2)
compliant, meek   **31 muffler** blindfold   **37 is make** has made
38 moral emblem   **39 Fortune . . . foe** (Probably alludes to the ballad
"Fortune, my foe!")

For he hath stolen a pax,   40
And hangèd must 'a be—a damnèd death!
Let gallows gape for dog; let man go free,
And let not hemp his windpipe suffocate.
But Exeter hath given the doom of death   44
For pax of little price.
Therefore, go speak—the Duke will hear thy voice—
And let not Bardolph's vital thread be cut
With edge of penny cord and vile reproach.   48
Speak, Captain, for his life, and I will thee requite.   49

FLUELLEN Aunchient Pistol, I do partly understand
  your meaning.

PISTOL Why then rejoice therefor.

FLUELLEN Certainly, Aunchient, it is not a thing to rejoice at. For if, look you, he were my brother, I would
  desire the Duke to use his good pleasure and put him
  to execution; for discipline ought to be used.

PISTOL
Die and be damned! And *figo* for thy friendship!   57

FLUELLEN It is well.

PISTOL The fig of Spain!   *Exit.*

FLUELLEN Very good.

GOWER Why, this is an arrant counterfeit rascal! I remember him now; a bawd, a cutpurse.

FLUELLEN I'll assure you, 'a uttered as prave words at
  the pridge as you shall see in a summer's day. But it is
  very well. What he has spoke to me, that is well, I
  warrant you, when time is serve.

GOWER Why, 'tis a gull, a fool, a rogue, that now and   67
  then goes to the wars to grace himself at his return
  into London under the form of a soldier. And such
  fellows are perfect in the great commanders' names,   70
  and they will learn you by rote where services were   71
  done—at such and such a sconce, at such a breach, at   72
  such a convoy; who came off bravely, who was shot,

---

40 pax metal disk with a crucifix stamped on it, kissed by the priest
during Mass. (But Holinshed describes an incident in which the object
stolen is a *pyx*, the vessel containing the consecrated host.) **44 doom**
judgment, sentence **48 cord** rope **49 requite** repay **57 figo** gesture of
contempt made by thrusting the thumb between the index and middle
fingers **67 gull** simpleton **70 are perfect in** i.e., can recite perfectly
71 learn teach **72 sconce** fortification

who disgraced, what terms the enemy stood on—and 74
this they con perfectly in the phrase of war, which 75
they trick up with new-tuned oaths. And what a beard 76
of the General's cut and a horrid suit of the camp will 77
do among foaming bottles and ale-washed wits is
wonderful to be thought on. But you must learn to
know such slanders of the age, or else you may be 80
marvelously mistook. 81

FLUELLEN   I tell you what, Captain Gower, I do perceive
he is not the man that he would gladly make show to
the world he is. If I find a hole in his coat, I will tell 84
him my mind. [*Drum heard.*] Hark you, the King is
coming, and I must speak with him from the pridge. 86

    Drum and colors. Enter the King and his poor
    soldiers [and Gloucester].

God pless Your Majesty!

KING   How now, Fluellen, cam'st thou from the
bridge?

FLUELLEN   Ay, so please Your Majesty. The Duke of Exeter has very gallantly maintained the pridge. The French
is gone off, look you, and there is gallant and most prave
passages. Marry, th' athversary was have possession of 93
the pridge, but he is enforced to retire, and the Duke of
Exeter is master of the pridge. I can tell Your Majesty,
the Duke is a prave man.

KING   What men have you lost, Fluellen?

FLUELLEN   The perdition of th' athversary hath been very 98
great, reasonable great. Marry, for my part, I think the
Duke hath lost never a man, but one that is like to be ex- 100
ecuted for robbing a church, one Bardolph, if Your Majesty know the man. His face is all bubukles, and whelks, 102
and knobs, and flames o' fire, and his lips blows at his
nose, and it is like a coal of fire, sometimes plue and

---

74 terms . . . stood on conditions the enemy insisted on   **75 con** learn
by heart   **76 trick** dress.   **new-tuned** i.e., of the latest fashion
77 horrid . . . camp fierce battle costume   **80 slanders of the age** persons who are a disgrace to the times   **81 mistook** mistaken, deluded
84 a hole . . . coat i.e., a weak spot in him. (Proverbial.)   **86 from the
pridge** with news concerning the bridge   **93 passages** deeds of arms.
was did   **98 perdition** losses   **100 like** likely   **102 bubukles** carbun-
cles.   **whelks** boils, pimples

sometimes red; but his nose is executed, and his fire's
out.

KING   We would have all such offenders so cut off. And we
give express charge that, in our marches through the
country, there be nothing compelled from the villages,
nothing taken but paid for, none of the French up-
braided or abused in disdainful language; for when lenity and cruelty play for a kingdom, the gentler gamester   112
is the soonest winner.   113

    Tucket. Enter Montjoy.

MONTJOY   You know me by my habit.   114
KING   Well then, I know thee. What shall I know of thee?
MONTJOY   My master's mind.
KING   Unfold it.
MONTJOY   Thus says my king: "Say thou to Harry of England, though we seemed dead, we did but sleep. Ad-   119
vantage is a better soldier than rashness. Tell him we   120
could have rebuked him at Harfleur, but that we
thought not good to bruise an injury till it were full   122
ripe. Now we speak upon our cue, and our voice is
imperial. England shall repent his folly, see his weak-   124
ness, and admire our sufferance. Bid him therefore   125
consider of his ransom, which must proportion the   126
losses we have borne, the subjects we have lost, the
disgrace we have digested; which in weight to re-   128
answer, his pettiness would bow under. For our losses,   129
his exchequer is too poor; for th' effusion of our blood, 130
the muster of his kingdom too faint a number; and for   131
our disgrace, his own person kneeling at our feet but
a weak and worthless satisfaction. To this add defiance; and tell him, for conclusion, he hath betrayed his
followers, whose condemnation is pronounced." So far   135
my King and master; so much my office.

112 gamester player   **113 s.d. Tucket** trumpet signal, fanfare
114 habit i.e., tabard, herald's coat   **119–120 Advantage** favorable
circumstance   **122 bruise an injury** i.e., squeeze a boil or pimple
124 England i.e., King Henry   **125 admire our sufferance** wonder at
our patience   **126 proportion** be proportional to   **128–129 which . . .
under** i.e., to compensate for which his means are too slender
130 exchequer treasury   **131 muster** total population
135 condemnation death sentence

KING
  What is thy name? I know thy quality.   137
MONTJOY   Montjoy.
KING
  Thou dost thy office fairly. Turn thee back,
  And tell thy King I do not seek him now,
  But could be willing to march on to Calais
  Without impeachment. For, to say the sooth,   142
  Though 'tis no wisdom to confess so much
  Unto an enemy of craft and vantage,   144
  My people are with sickness much enfeebled,
  My numbers lessened, and those few I have
  Almost no better than so many French,
  Who when they were in health, I tell thee, herald,
  I thought upon one pair of English legs
  Did march three Frenchmen. Yet, forgive me, God,
  That I do brag thus! This your air of France
  Hath blown that vice in me. I must repent.   152
  Go, therefore, tell thy master here I am;
  My ransom is this frail and worthless trunk,   154
  My army but a weak and sickly guard.
  Yet, God before, tell him we will come on,
  Though France himself and such another neighbor
  Stand in our way. There's for thy labor, Montjoy.
                     [*He gives a purse.*]
  Go bid thy master well advise himself.   159
  If we may pass, we will; if we be hindered,
  We shall your tawny ground with your red blood
  Discolor. And so, Montjoy, fare you well.
  The sum of all our answer is but this:
  We would not seek a battle as we are,
  Nor, as we are, we say we will not shun it.
  So tell your master.
MONTJOY
  I shall deliver so. Thanks to Your Highness.   [*Exit.*]
GLOUCESTER
  I hope they will not come upon us now.
KING
  We are in God's hand, brother, not in theirs.

137 quality rank and profession   **142 impeachment** impediment.   **sooth**
truth   **144 vantage** superiority in resources   **152 blown** brought to
bloom   **154 trunk** body   **159 advise himself** consider

March to the bridge. It now draws toward night.
Beyond the river we'll encamp ourselves,
And on tomorrow bid them march away.   *Exeunt.* 172

❖

3.7   *Enter the Constable of France, the Lord*
          Rambures, Orleans, Dauphin, with others.

CONSTABLE Tut, I have the best armor of the world.
  Would it were day!
ORLEANS You have an excellent armor; but let my horse
  have his due.
CONSTABLE It is the best horse of Europe.
ORLEANS Will it never be morning?
DAUPHIN My lord of Orleans and my Lord High Con-
  stable, you talk of horse and armor?
ORLEANS You are as well provided of both as any prince
  in the world.
DAUPHIN What a long night is this! I will not change
  my horse with any that treads but on four pasterns. 12
  Ça, ha! He bounds from the earth as if his entrails 13
  were hairs; *le cheval volant*, the Pegasus, *qui a les na-* 14
  rines de feu! When I bestride him, I soar, I am a hawk. 15
  He trots the air. The earth sings when he touches it.
  The basest horn of his hoof is more musical than the 17
  pipe of Hermes. 18
ORLEANS He's of the color of the nutmeg.
DAUPHIN And of the heat of the ginger. It is a beast for
  Perseus. He is pure air and fire; and the dull elements 21
  of earth and water never appear in him, but only in

---

172 **bid . . . away** i.e., bid our army march toward Calais

3.7. Location: The French camp, near Agincourt.
12 **pasterns** i.e., hooves. (The *pastern* literally is the part of the horse's
leg between the fetlock and the hoof.) **13–14 as . . . hairs** i.e., as if he
were a tennis ball. (Tennis balls were stuffed with hair.) **14–15 le cheval
. . . feu** the flying horse, Pegasus, with nostrils breathing fire **17 basest
horn** (1) lowest part (2) hoofbeat **18 pipe of Hermes** (Hermes, messenger of the gods, charmed Argus of the hundred eyes asleep with playing
on his pipe.) **21 Perseus** (According to some Greek legends and to Ovid,
Perseus rode Pegasus when he rescued Andromeda from the dragon.)

patient stillness while his rider mounts him. He is indeed a horse, and all other jades you may call beasts.

CONSTABLE   Indeed, my lord, it is a most absolute and 25
excellent horse.

DAUPHIN   It is the prince of palfreys. His neigh is like 27
the bidding of a monarch, and his countenance enforces homage.

ORLEANS   No more, cousin.

DAUPHIN   Nay, the man hath no wit that cannot, from
the rising of the lark to the lodging of the lamb, vary 32
deserved praise on my palfrey. It is a theme as fluent
as the sea; turn the sands into eloquent tongues, and
my horse is argument for them all. 'Tis a subject for a 35
sovereign to reason on, and for a sovereign's sovereign 36
to ride on; and for the world, familiar to us and un- 37
known, to lay apart their particular functions and 38
wonder at him. I once writ a sonnet in his praise, and 39
began thus: "Wonder of nature"—

ORLEANS   I have heard a sonnet begin so to one's mistress.

DAUPHIN   Then did they imitate that which I composed
to my courser, for my horse is my mistress.   44

ORLEANS   Your mistress bears well.

DAUPHIN   Me well, which is the prescript praise and 46
perfection of a good and particular mistress.   47

CONSTABLE   Nay, for methought yesterday your mistress shrewdly shook your back.   49

DAUPHIN   So perhaps did yours.

CONSTABLE   Mine was not bridled.   51

DAUPHIN   O, then belike she was old and gentle, and 52
you rode like a kern of Ireland, your French hose off, 53
and in your strait strossers.   54

---

25 absolute perfect   **27 palfreys** saddle horses   **32 lodging** lying down.
vary produce variations of   **35 argument** subject   **36 reason** discourse
37–39 for . . . him for both the known and unknown worlds to put aside
their differences and join in wondering at him (the horse)   **44 horse is my
mistress** (Here begins a series of bawdy double entendres involving
human and animal sexuality: *bears, shook your back, rode, foul bogs,
doing,* etc.)   **46 prescript** prescribed   **47 particular** acknowledging only
one master   **49 shrewdly** viciously   **51 Mine . . . bridled** i.e., at least my
mistress was not a horse   **52 belike** probably   **53 kern** Irish foot soldier.
(Here used to mean "rustic" or "boor.")   **French hose** wide breeches
54 strait strossers tight trousers, i.e., barelegged

CONSTABLE   You have good judgment in horsemanship.

DAUPHIN   Be warned by me, then: they that ride so, and ride not warily, fall into foul bogs. I had rather have my horse to my mistress.   58

CONSTABLE   I had as lief have my mistress a jade.   59

DAUPHIN   I tell thee, Constable, my mistress wears his   60
own hair.   61

CONSTABLE   I could make as true a boast as that if I had a sow to my mistress.

DAUPHIN   *"Le chien est retourné à son propre vomisse-*   64
ment, et la truie lavée au bourbier." Thou mak'st use   65
of anything.

CONSTABLE   Yet do I not use my horse for my mistress, or any such proverb so little kin to the purpose.   68

RAMBURES   My Lord Constable, the armor that I saw in your tent tonight, are those stars or suns upon it?

CONSTABLE   Stars, my lord.

DAUPHIN   Some of them will fall tomorrow, I hope.

CONSTABLE   And yet my sky shall not want.   73

DAUPHIN   That may be, for you bear a many superflu-   74
ously, and 'twere more honor some were away.   75

CONSTABLE   Even as your horse bears your praises, who would trot as well were some of your brags dismounted.

DAUPHIN   Would I were able to load him with his desert! Will it never be day? I will trot tomorrow a mile, and my way shall be paved with English faces.

CONSTABLE   I will not say so, for fear I should be faced   82
out of my way. But I would it were morning, for I   83
would fain be about the ears of the English.   84

RAMBURES   Who will go to hazard with me for twenty   85
prisoners?

58 to as   **59 lief** happily   **60–61 wears ... hair** i.e., is not artificially wigged, like an elegant court lady, and perhaps bald from syphilis **64–65 Le chien ... bourbier** the dog is returned to his own vomit, and the washed sow to the mire. (See 2 Peter 2:22.)   **68 kin** related   **73 sky** i.e., sky of honor.   **want** be lacking (in honor)   **74 a many** i.e., many. (Parallel to "a few.")   **75 'twere ... away** i.e., it would be more honest and proper if some of your stars were done away with   **82–83 faced ... way** braved out of my way, put to shame   **84 fain** gladly.   **about the ears** buffeting the heads   **85 go to hazard** bet, play at dice. (But the Constable replies in the sense of "encounter danger.")

CONSTABLE   You must first go yourself to hazard ere you have them.

DAUPHIN   'Tis midnight; I'll go arm myself.   *Exit.*

ORLEANS   The Dauphin longs for morning.

RAMBURES   He longs to eat the English.

CONSTABLE   I think he will eat all he kills.

ORLEANS   By the white hand of my lady, he's a gallant prince.

CONSTABLE   Swear by her foot, that she may tread out the oath.   95 96

ORLEANS   He is simply the most active gentleman of France.

CONSTABLE   Doing is activity, and he will still be doing.   99

ORLEANS   He never did harm, that I heard of.   100

CONSTABLE   Nor will do none tomorrow. He will keep that good name still.

ORLEANS   I know him to be valiant.

CONSTABLE   I was told that by one that knows him better than you.

ORLEANS   What's he?

CONSTABLE   Marry, he told me so himself, and he said he cared not who knew it.

ORLEANS   He needs not; it is no hidden virtue in him.   109

CONSTABLE   By my faith, sir, but it is. Never anybody saw it but his lackey. 'Tis a hooded valor, and when it appears it will bate.   110 111 112

ORLEANS   Ill will never said well.

CONSTABLE   I will cap that proverb with "There is flattery in friendship."

ORLEANS   And I will take up that with "Give the devil his due."   116 117

95–96 tread . . . oath (1) fulfill the oath by dancing (2) stamp on, spurn the oath   **99 Doing** i.e., acting, pretending.   **still** continually   **100 did harm** i.e., offended. (But the Constable uses it to mean "hurt any enemy.")   **109 He needs not** i.e., there is no need for him to proclaim it himself.   **it** i.e., valor   **110–111 Never . . . lackey** i.e., he shows "valor" only in beating his servant   **111 hooded valor** (The hawk was kept hooded to prevent it from beating its wings, or "bating.")   **112 bate** (1) beat its wings (2) abate, be downcast   **116–117 Give . . . due** give even the devil his due, allow praise even to those who criticize. (But the Constable turns this proverb against the Dauphin by likening him to the devil.)

CONSTABLE   Well placed. There stands your friend for   118
the devil. Have at the very eye of that proverb with   119
"A pox of the devil."

ORLEANS   You are the better at proverbs by how much
"A fool's bolt is soon shot."   122

CONSTABLE   You have shot over.   123

ORLEANS   'Tis not the first time you were overshot.   124

Enter a Messenger.

MESSENGER   My Lord High Constable, the English lie
within fifteen hundred paces of your tents.

CONSTABLE   Who hath measured the ground?

MESSENGER   The Lord Grandpré.

CONSTABLE   A valiant and most expert gentleman.
[*Exit Messenger.*] Would it were day! Alas, poor Harry of
England! He longs not for the dawning as we do.

ORLEANS   What a wretched and peevish fellow is this
King of England, to mope with his fat-brained follow-   133
ers so far out of his knowledge!

CONSTABLE   If the English had any apprehension, they   135
would run away.

ORLEANS   That they lack; for if their heads had any in-
tellectual armor, they could never wear such heavy
headpieces.

RAMBURES   That island of England breeds very valiant
creatures; their mastiffs are of unmatchable courage.

ORLEANS   Foolish curs, that run winking into the mouth   142
of a Russian bear and have their heads crushed like
rotten apples. You may as well say "That's a valiant flea
that dare eat his breakfast on the lip of a lion."

CONSTABLE   Just, just! And the men do sympathize with   146
the mastiffs in robustious and rough coming on, leav-   147
ing their wits with their wives; and then give them
great meals of beef, and iron and steel, they will eat like

118–119 There . . . devil i.e., you just called the Dauphin the devil.
119 Have . . . eye shoot straight at the mark. (A sporting term appropriate to this verbal contest of "capping proverbs.")   **122 bolt** short, blunt
arrow   **123 shot over** i.e., shot over the mark   **124 overshot** i.e., out-
shot, defeated   **133 mope** (1) wander about (2) be downcast
135 apprehension (1) sense (2) sense of danger   **142 winking** shut-
ting their eyes   **146 Just** exactly.   **sympathize with** resemble
147 robustious violent, boisterous

wolves and fight like devils.

ORLEANS Ay, but these English are shrewdly out of 151
beef.

CONSTABLE Then shall we find tomorrow they have
only stomachs to eat and none to fight. Now is it time 154
to arm. Come, shall we about it?

ORLEANS
It is now two o'clock; but let me see, by ten
We shall have each a hundred Englishmen.   *Exeunt.*

❖

4.0   [*Enter*] *Chorus.*

CHORUS

Now entertain conjecture of a time   1
When creeping murmur and the poring dark   2
Fills the wide vessel of the universe.
From camp to camp, through the foul womb of night,
The hum of either army stilly sounds,   5
That the fixed sentinels almost receive
The secret whispers of each other's watch.
Fire answers fire, and through their paly flames   8
Each battle sees the other's umbered face.   9
Steed threatens steed, in high and boastful neighs
Piercing the night's dull ear; and from the tents
The armorers, accomplishing the knights,   12
With busy hammers closing rivets up,
Give dreadful note of preparation.
The country cocks do crow, the clocks do toll,
And the third hour of drowsy morning name.
Proud of their numbers and secure in soul,   17
The confident and overlusty French   18
Do the low-rated English play at dice,   19
And chide the cripple tardy-gaited night,
Who like a foul and ugly witch doth limp
So tediously away. The poor condemnèd English,
Like sacrifices, by their watchful fires
Sit patiently and inly ruminate   24
The morning's danger; and their gesture sad,   25
Investing lank-lean cheeks and war-worn coats, 26
Presenteth them unto the gazing moon
So many horrid ghosts. O, now, who will behold
The royal captain of this ruined band
Walking from watch to watch, from tent to tent,
Let him cry, "Praise and glory on his head!"
For forth he goes and visits all his host,   32

4.0. Chorus.
1 entertain conjecture of i.e., imagine **2 poring** in which one must strain the eyes to see **5 stilly** softly **8 paly** pale **9 battle** army. **umbered** shadowed **12 accomplishing** equipping **17 secure** overconfident **18 overlusty** overly merry **19 play** gamble for **24 inly** inwardly **25 gesture sad** serious bearing **26 Investing** clothing **32 host** army

Bids them good morrow with a modest smile,
And calls them brothers, friends, and countrymen.
Upon his royal face there is no note
How dread an army hath enrounded him.   36
Nor doth he dedicate one jot of color   37
Unto the weary and all-watchèd night,   38
But freshly looks and overbears attaint   39
With cheerful semblance and sweet majesty;
That every wretch, pining and pale before,
Beholding him, plucks comfort from his looks.
A largess universal like the sun
His liberal eye doth give to everyone,
Thawing cold fear, that mean and gentle all   45
Behold, as may unworthiness define,   46
A little touch of Harry in the night.
And so our scene must to the battle fly;
Where—O, for pity!—we shall much disgrace
With four or five most vile and ragged foils,
Right ill-disposed in brawl ridiculous,
The name of Agincourt. Yet sit and see,
Minding true things by what their mockeries be.   53

Exit.

4.1   *Enter the King, Bedford, and Gloucester.*

KING
  Gloucester, 'tis true that we are in great danger;
  The greater therefore should our courage be.
  Good morrow, brother Bedford. God Almighty!
  There is some soul of goodness in things evil,
  Would men observingly distill it out;   5

36 enrounded surrounded   **37 dedicate** yield up.   **color** i.e., bright
color of complexion   **38 all-watchèd** spent entirely in wakefulness and
waiting   **39 overbears attaint** overcomes the effects of weariness and
depression   **45 mean and gentle** those of low and of high birth   **46 as
. . . define** as we can express to you only imperfectly   **53 Minding**
bearing in mind.   **mockeries** inadequate imitations

4.1. Location: The English camp at Agincourt.
5 observingly observantly

For our bad neighbor makes us early stirrers,
Which is both healthful and good husbandry.   7
Besides, they are our outward consciences
And preachers to us all, admonishing
That we should dress us fairly for our end.   10
Thus may we gather honey from the weed
And make a moral of the devil himself.

    Enter Erpingham.

Good morrow, old Sir Thomas Erpingham.
A good soft pillow for that good white head
Were better than a churlish turf of France.   15

ERPINGHAM
  Not so, my liege. This lodging likes me better,   16
Since I may say, "Now lie I like a king."

KING
  'Tis good for men to love their present pains
Upon example; so the spirit is eased.   19
And when the mind is quickened, out of doubt
The organs, though defunct and dead before,
Break up their drowsy grave and newly move   22
With casted slough and fresh legerity.   23
Lend me thy cloak, Sir Thomas. [*The King puts on
  Erpingham's cloak.*] Brothers both,   24
Commend me to the princes in our camp;
Do my good morrow to them, and anon
Desire them all to my pavilion.

GLOUCESTER We shall, my liege.

ERPINGHAM Shall I attend Your Grace?

KING No, my good knight,
Go with my brothers to my lords of England.
I and my bosom must debate awhile,
And then I would no other company.

ERPINGHAM
  The Lord in heaven bless thee, noble Harry!
                         Exeunt [all but King].

---

7 husbandry economy, thrift   **10 dress us fairly** prepare ourselves well
15 churlish rough, hard   **16 likes** pleases   **19 Upon example** i.e., following
or considering the example of persons such as King Henry and Er-
pingham   **22 Break . . . grave** i.e., break out of their lethargy   **23 With
casted slough** i.e., as though having cast off its old skin, like a snake.
legerity nimbleness   **24 Brothers both** i.e., Bedford and Gloucester

KING
  God-a-mercy, old heart! Thou speak'st cheerfully.

    Enter Pistol.

PISTOL   *Che vous là?*   36
KING   A friend.
PISTOL
  Discuss unto me: art thou officer,   38
  Or art thou base, common, and popular?   39
KING   I am a gentleman of a company.
PISTOL   Trail'st thou the puissant pike?   41
KING   Even so. What are you?
PISTOL
  As good a gentleman as the Emperor.   43
KING   Then you are a better than the King.
PISTOL
  The King's a bawcock and a heart of gold,   45
  A lad of life, an imp of fame,   46
  Of parents good, of fist most valiant.
  I kiss his dirty shoe, and from heartstring
  I love the lovely bully. What is thy name?   49
KING   Harry le Roy.
PISTOL
  Le Roy? A Cornish name. Art thou of Cornish crew?
KING   No, I am a Welshman.   52
PISTOL   Know'st thou Fluellen?
KING   Yes.
PISTOL
  Tell him I'll knock his leek about his pate   55
  Upon Saint Davy's Day.   56
KING   Do not you wear your dagger in your cap that
  day, lest he knock that about yours.
PISTOL   Art thou his friend?

36 Che vous là i.e., *qui va là,* who goes there; or *qui vous là,* who are
you there. (Pistol's imperfect French.)   **38 Discuss** declare   **39 popular**
of low birth   **41 Trail'st . . . pike** i.e., are you in the infantry
43 Emperor i.e., Holy Roman Emperor   **45 bawcock** fine fellow. (From
French *beau coq*.)   **46 imp of fame** child or scion of renown   **49 bully**
(A term of endearment meaning "fine fellow.")   **52 Welshman** (Henry
was born at Monmouth, then considered part of Wales.)   **55–56 leek . . .
Day** (On Saint David's Day, March 1, the leek was worn in memory of a
Welsh victory over the Saxons, since Saint David, the Welsh leader, had
commanded his followers to wear leeks in their caps on that occasion.)

KING   And his kinsman too.
PISTOL   The *figo* for thee, then!   61
KING   I thank you. God be with you!
PISTOL   My name is Pistol called.   *Exit.*
KING   It sorts well with your fierceness.   64
                          Manet King [standing apart].

          Enter Fluellen and Gower [meeting].

GOWER   Captain Fluellen!
FLUELLEN   So, in the name of Jesu Christ, speak fewer.   66
   It is the greatest admiration in the universal world,   67
   when the true and aunchient prerogatifes and laws of
   the wars is not kept. If you would take the pains but
   to examine the wars of Pompey the Great, you shall   70
   find, I warrant you, that there is no tiddle-taddle nor   71
   pibble-pabble in Pompey's camp. I warrant you, you   72
   shall find the ceremonies of the wars, and the cares of
   it, and the forms of it, and the sobriety of it, and the 74
   modesty of it, to be otherwise.   75
GOWER   Why, the enemy is loud; you hear him all
   night.
FLUELLEN   If the enemy is an ass and a fool and a prating   78
   coxcomb, is it meet, think you, that we should also,   79
   look you, be an ass and a fool and a prating coxcomb?
   In your own conscience, now?
GOWER   I will speak lower.
FLUELLEN   I pray you and beseech you that you will.
                          Exit [with Gower].
KING
   Though it appear a little out of fashion,
   There is much care and valor in this Welshman.

          *Enter three soldiers, John Bates, Alexander Court,
          and Michael Williams.*

COURT   Brother John Bates, is not that the morning
   which breaks yonder?

61 figo (A provoking gesture of contempt; see 3.6.57, note.)   **64 sorts** fits,
agrees   **s.d. Manet King** the King remains   **66 fewer** i.e., calmly,
more quietly   **67 admiration** wonder   **70 Pompey the Great** Roman
general defeated by Julius Caesar   **71–72 tiddle-taddle nor pibble-
pabble** tittle-tattle nor bibble-babble   **74 sobriety** orderliness, deco-
rum   **75 modesty** propriety   **78–79 prating coxcomb** chattering fool

BATES　I think it be. But we have no great cause to desire the approach of day.

WILLIAMS　We see yonder the beginning of the day, but I think we shall never see the end of it.—Who goes there?

KING　A friend.

WILLIAMS　Under what captain serve you?

KING　Under Sir Thomas Erpingham.

WILLIAMS　A good old commander and a most kind gentleman. I pray you, what thinks he of our estate? 97

KING　Even as men wrecked upon a sand, that look to be 98 washed off the next tide.

BATES　He hath not told his thought to the King?

KING　No, nor it is not meet he should. For, though I 101 speak it to you, I think the King is but a man, as I am. The violet smells to him as it doth to me; the element 103 shows to him as it doth to me; all his senses have but 104 human conditions. His ceremonies laid by, in his na- 105 kedness he appears but a man; and though his affec- 106 tions are higher mounted than ours, yet when they 107 stoop, they stoop with the like wing. Therefore when he sees reason of fears, as we do, his fears, out of doubt, be of the same relish as ours are. Yet, in reason, 110 no man should possess him with any appearance of 111 fear, lest he, by showing it, should dishearten his army.

BATES　He may show what outward courage he will; but I believe, as cold a night as 'tis, he could wish himself in Thames up to the neck; and so I would he were, and I by him, at all adventures, so we were quit here. 117

KING　By my troth, I will speak my conscience of the King: I think he would not wish himself anywhere but where he is.

BATES　Then I would he were here alone. So should he

---

97 estate condition　**98 wrecked** shipwrecked　**101 meet** fitting
103–104 element shows sky appears　**105 conditions** qualities, i.e., limitations. **ceremonies** observances due royalty; royal robes　**106–107 affections . . . mounted** desires soar higher. (A falconry metaphor continued in *stoop*, descend, swoop down, and *with the like wing*, similarly.)
110 relish taste　**111 possess him with** induce in him　**117 at all adventures** at all events (since the Thames would be less risky under any circumstances than the impending battle). **quit here** out of this situation

be sure to be ransomed, and a many poor men's lives
saved.

KING   I dare say you love him not so ill to wish him here
alone, howsoever you speak this to feel other men's
minds. Methinks I could not die anywhere so contented as in the King's company, his cause being just
and his quarrel honorable.

WILLIAMS   That's more than we know.

BATES   Ay, or more than we should seek after; for we
know enough if we know we are the King's subjects.
If his cause be wrong, our obedience to the King
wipes the crime of it out of us.

WILLIAMS   But if the cause be not good, the King himself hath a heavy reckoning to make, when all those
legs and arms and heads, chopped off in a battle, shall
join together at the Latter Day and cry all, "We died at   137
such a place"—some swearing, some crying for a sur-
geon, some upon their wives left poor behind them,
some upon the debts they owe, some upon their children rawly left. I am afeard there are few die well that   141
die in a battle; for how can they charitably dispose of
anything, when blood is their argument? Now, if
these men do not die well, it will be a black matter for
the King that led them to it; who to disobey were   145
against all proportion of subjection.   146

KING   So, if a son that is by his father sent about mer-
chandise do sinfully miscarry upon the sea, the im-   148
putation of his wickedness, by your rule, should be   149
imposed upon his father that sent him; or if a servant,
under his master's command transporting a sum of
money, be assailed by robbers and die in many irrec-   152
onciled iniquities, you may call the business of the   153
master the author of the servant's damnation. But this
is not so. The King is not bound to answer the partic-   155
ular endings of his soldiers, the father of his son, nor
the master of his servant; for they purpose not their   157
deaths when they propose their services. Besides,

---

137 **Latter Day** last day, Day of Judgment   141 **rawly** without provi-
sion   145 **who** whom   146 **proportion of subjection** proper duty of a
subject   148 **sinfully miscarry** die in his sins   148–149 **imputation**
charge, accusation   152–153 **in . . . iniquities** with his wicked deeds
unabsolved   155 **answer** answer for   157 **purpose** intend

there is no king, be his cause never so spotless, if it
come to the arbitrament of swords, can try it out with 160
all unspotted soldiers. Some, peradventure, have on 161
them the guilt of premeditated and contrived murder;
some, of beguiling virgins with the broken seals of
perjury; some, making the wars their bulwark, that 164
have before gored the gentle bosom of peace with pillage and robbery. Now, if these men have defeated 166
the law and outrun native punishment, though they 167
can outstrip men, they have no wings to fly from God.
War is his beadle, war is his vengeance; so that here 169
men are punished for before-breach of the King's laws 170
in now the King's quarrel. Where they feared the 171
death, they have borne life away; and where they 172
would be safe, they perish. Then if they die unpro- 173
vided, no more is the King guilty of their damnation 174
than he was before guilty of those impieties for the
which they are now visited. Every subject's duty is the 176
King's; but every subject's soul is his own. Therefore
should every soldier in the wars do as every sick man
in his bed, wash every mote out of his conscience; and 179
dying so, death is to him advantage, or not dying, the
time was blessedly lost wherein such preparation was
gained. And in him that escapes, it were not sin to
think that, making God so free an offer, He let him
outlive that day to see His greatness and to teach others how they should prepare.

WILLIAMS 'Tis certain, every man that dies ill, the ill 186
upon his own head, the King is not to answer it.

BATES I do not desire he should answer for me, and yet
I determine to fight lustily for him.

KING I myself heard the King say he would not be ransomed.

WILLIAMS Ay, he said so, to make us fight cheerfully;

---

160 arbitrament arbitration **161 unspotted** innocent **164 bulwark**
refuge from punishment (for offenses committed) **166 defeated** broken **167 native** at home **169 beadle** parish officer responsible for
punishing petty offenders **170 before-breach** prior violation
171–173 Where . . . perish i.e., whereas before they feared execution but
escaped punishment, here where they look for safety they die in battle
173–174 unprovided spiritually unprepared **176 visited** i.e., by punishment **179 mote** small impurity **186 dies ill** dies in sin

but when our throats are cut, he may be ransomed
and we ne'er the wiser.

KING If I live to see it, I will never trust his word after.

WILLIAMS You pay him then! That's a perilous shot out 196
of an elder-gun, that a poor and a private displeasure 197
can do against a monarch. You may as well go about
to turn the sun to ice with fanning in his face with a
peacock's feather. You'll never trust his word after!
Come, 'tis a foolish saying.

KING Your reproof is something too round. I should be 202
angry with you, if the time were convenient.

WILLIAMS Let it be a quarrel between us, if you live.

KING I embrace it.

WILLIAMS How shall I know thee again?

KING Give me any gage of thine, and I will wear it in 207
my bonnet. Then if ever thou dar'st acknowledge it,
I will make it my quarrel.

WILLIAMS Here's my glove. Give me another of thine.

KING There.   [*They exchange gloves.*]

WILLIAMS This will I also wear in my cap. If ever thou
come to me and say, after tomorrow, "This is my
glove," by this hand, I will take thee a box on the ear. 214

KING If ever I live to see it, I will challenge it.

WILLIAMS Thou dar'st as well be hanged.

KING Well, I will do it, though I take thee in the King's
company.

WILLIAMS Keep thy word. Fare thee well.

BATES Be friends, you English fools, be friends. We
have French quarrels enough, if you could tell how to 221
reckon.

KING Indeed, the French may lay twenty French crowns 223
to one they will beat us, for they bear them on their
shoulders; but it is no English treason to cut French 225
crowns, and tomorrow the King himself will be a
clipper.   *Exeunt soldiers.*

---

196 You pay him then i.e., that will really pay him back for his perfidy,
won't it. (Said sarcastically.) **197 elder-gun** popgun made from a
branch of elder with the pith hollowed out **202 round** direct,
brusque **207 gage** pledge **214 take** give, strike **221 could tell** knew
223 crowns (1) coins (2) heads **225 English treason** (It was a treason-
able offense to clip or "cut" English coins; it obviously is no offense to
slash French heads, and even King Henry will be such a "clipper.")

Upon the King! Let us our lives, our souls,
Our debts, our careful wives,   229
Our children, and our sins lay on the King!
We must bear all. O hard condition,
Twin-born with greatness, subject to the breath   232
Of every fool, whose sense no more can feel   233
But his own wringing! What infinite heartsease   234
Must kings neglect that private men enjoy!
And what have kings that privates have not too,   236
Save ceremony, save general ceremony?
And what art thou, thou idol ceremony?
What kind of god art thou, that suffer'st more
Of mortal griefs than do thy worshipers?
What are thy rents? What are thy comings-in?   241
O ceremony, show me but thy worth!
What is thy soul of adoration?   243
Art thou aught else but place, degree, and form,   244
Creating awe and fear in other men?
Wherein thou art less happy, being feared,
Than they in fearing.
What drink'st thou oft, instead of homage sweet,
But poisoned flattery? O, be sick, great greatness,
And bid thy ceremony give thee cure!
Thinks thou the fiery fever will go out   251
With titles blown from adulation?   252
Will it give place to flexure and low bending?   253
Canst thou, when thou command'st the beggar's knee,
Command the health of it? No, thou proud dream,
That play'st so subtly with a king's repose.
I am a king that find thee, and I know   257
'Tis not the balm, the scepter, and the ball,   258
The sword, the mace, the crown imperial,   259

229 **careful** full of cares   232–234 **Twin-born . . . wringing** i.e., inseparable
from the condition of being born of royal rank, a condition that makes one
the subject of the idle gossip of every fool, even those whose sensibilities
pay attention to nothing other than the rumbling of their own stomachs
236 **privates** private men   241 **comings-in** revenues   243 **thy soul of
adoration** the essential quality that makes you so much admired
244 **place** rank   251–252 **will . . . adulation** will be extinguished by
speeches breathed by flatterers   253 **it give place to flexure** it (a fever,
illness) yield to bowing   257 **find** expose   258 **balm** consecrating oil used
to anoint a king in his coronation   259 **mace** ceremonial staff

The intertissued robe of gold and pearl,   260
The farcèd title running 'fore the king,   261
The throne he sits on, nor the tide of pomp
That beats upon the high shore of this world—
No, not all these, thrice-gorgeous ceremony,
Not all these, laid in bed majestical,
Can sleep so soundly as the wretched slave
Who, with a body filled and vacant mind,
Gets him to rest, crammed with distressful bread;   268
Never sees horrid night, the child of hell,
But like a lackey from the rise to set   270
Sweats in the eye of Phoebus, and all night   271
Sleeps in Elysium; next day after dawn   272
Doth rise and help Hyperion to his horse,   273
And follows so the ever-running year
With profitable labor to his grave.
And but for ceremony, such a wretch,
Winding up days with toil and nights with sleep,
Had the forehand and vantage of a king.   278
The slave, a member of the country's peace,   279
Enjoys it; but in gross brain little wots   280
What watch the King keeps to maintain the peace,   281
Whose hours the peasant best advantages.   282

    Enter Erpingham.

ERPINGHAM
  My lord, your nobles, jealous of your absence,   283
  Seek through your camp to find you.
KING   Good old knight,
  Collect them all together at my tent.
  I'll be before thee.
ERPINGHAM   I shall do 't, my lord.   *Exit.* 286
KING
  O God of battles, steel my soldiers' hearts;

260 intertissued interwoven   **261 farcèd** stuffed (with pompous
phrases)   **268 distressful** earned by hard work   **270 lackey** constant
attendant.   **rise to set** sunrise to sunset   **271 Phoebus** the sun god
272 Elysium in Greek mythology, the abode of the blessed
273 Hyperion the charioteer of the sun. (The peasant is up before the
sun.)   **278 Had** would have.   **forehand** upper hand   **279 member**
sharer   **280 it** i.e., peace.   **wots** knows   **281 watch** wakeful guard
282 the peasant best advantages most benefit the peasant   **283 jealous
of** apprehensive because of   **286 be** be there

Possess them not with fear! Take from them now
The sense of reckoning, ere th' opposèd numbers   289
Pluck their hearts from them. Not today, O Lord,
O, not today, think not upon the fault   291
My father made in compassing the crown!   292
I Richard's body have interrèd new,   293
And on it have bestowed more contrite tears
Than from it issued forcèd drops of blood.
Five hundred poor I have in yearly pay
Who twice a day their withered hands hold up
Toward heaven, to pardon blood; and I have built
Two chantries, where the sad and solemn priests   299
Sing still for Richard's soul. More will I do;   300
Though all that I can do is nothing worth,
Since that my penitence comes after all,   302
Imploring pardon.

    Enter Gloucester.

GLOUCESTER My liege!
KING My brother Gloucester's voice? Ay;
  I know thy errand. I will go with thee.
  The day, my friends, and all things stay for me.

                              Exeunt.

❖

4.2   *Enter the Dauphin, Orleans, Rambures, and*
       others.

ORLEANS
  The sun doth gild our armor. Up, my lords!
DAUPHIN *Monte cheval!* My horse! *Varlet! Lacquais!* Ha! 2
ORLEANS O brave spirit!

---

289 sense of reckoning ability to count (the enemy) **291 the fault** i.e.,
the deposition and murder of Richard II **292 compassing** obtaining
293 new anew **299 chantries** chapels in which masses for the dead
were celebrated. **sad** grave **300 still** continually **302 Since that** i.e.,
as shown by the fact that

4.2. Location: The French camp.
s.d. others (The Folio text mentions Lord Beaumont but does not give
him a speaking part.) **2 Monte cheval** to horse

DAUPHIN *Via, les eaux et terre!*   4
ORLEANS *Rien puis? L'air et feu?*   5
DAUPHIN *Cieux*, cousin Orleans.   6

   Enter Constable.

  Now, my Lord Constable!
CONSTABLE
  Hark, how our steeds for present service neigh!   8
DAUPHIN
  Mount them and make incision in their hides,   9
  That their hot blood may spin in English eyes   10
  And dout them with superfluous courage. Ha!   11
RAMBURES
  What, will you have them weep our horses' blood?
  How shall we then behold their natural tears?

   Enter Messenger.

MESSENGER
  The English are embattled, you French peers.   14
CONSTABLE
  To horse, you gallant princes, straight to horse!
  Do but behold yond poor and starvèd band,
  And your fair show shall suck away their souls,   17
  Leaving them but the shales and husks of men.   18
  There is not work enough for all our hands,
  Scarce blood enough in all their sickly veins
  To give each naked curtal ax a stain   21
  That our French gallants shall today draw out
  And sheathe for lack of sport. Let us but blow on them,
  The vapor of our valor will o'erturn them.
  'Tis positive against all exceptions, lords,   25
  That our superfluous lackeys and our peasants,
  Who in unnecessary action swarm

---

4 Via . . . terre begone, waters and earth. (The Dauphin imagines himself
riding above rivers and solid ground.) **5 Rien . . . feu** nothing more?
What about air and fire? (i.e., Why not soar above all four elements, not
just water and earth?) **6 Cieux** the heavens. (The Dauphin carries the
metaphor one step further to its ultimate height.) **8 service** action
9 incision i.e., with spurs **10 spin** gush, spatter **11 And . . . courage** i.e.,
and put out the English eyes with the horses' superfluous blood, the
proof of their excessive courage. **dout** put out **14 embattled** arranged
in battle order **17 fair show** impressive appearance **18 shales** shells
21 curtal ax cutlass, short sword **25 exceptions** objections

About our squares of battle, were enough   28
To purge this field of such a hilding foe,   29
Though we upon this mountain's basis by   30
Took stand for idle speculation—   31
But that our honors must not. What's to say?   32
A very little little let us do
And all is done. Then let the trumpets sound
The tucket sonance and the note to mount;   35
For our approach shall so much dare the field   36
That England shall couch down in fear and yield.

    Enter Grandpré.

GRANDPRÉ
Why do you stay so long, my lords of France?
Yond island carrions, desperate of their bones,   39
Ill-favoredly become the morning field.   40
Their ragged curtains poorly are let loose,   41
And our air shakes them passing scornfully.   42
Big Mars seems bankrupt in their beggared host   43
And faintly through a rusty beaver peeps.   44
The horsemen sit like fixèd candlesticks,
With torch staves in their hand, and their poor jades 46
Lob down their heads, drooping the hides and hips,   47
The gum down-roping from their pale-dead eyes,   48
And in their pale dull mouths the gimmaled bit   49
Lies foul with chewed grass, still and motionless;
And their executors, the knavish crows,   51
Fly o'er them all impatient for their hour.
Description cannot suit itself in words
To demonstrate the life of such a battle   54
In life so lifeless as it shows itself.

---

28 squares of battle four-sided military formation   **29 hilding** worthless, base   **30 basis** foot.   **by** nearby   **31 speculation** looking on
32 But that except for the fact that   **35 tucket sonance** trumpet call
36 dare (1) defy (2) stupify with fear   **39 carrions** skeletons, cadavers.
desperate of without hope of saving   **40 Ill-favoredly become** i.e., are an
eyesore to   **41 curtains** colors, banners   **42 passing** exceedingly
43 Mars the god of war   **44 beaver** visor   **46 torch staves** i.e., tapers in
place of lances. (The horsemen themselves look like carved candle-
holders.)   **47 Lob down** hang down.   **drooping** letting droop   **48 gum**
watery discharge.   **down-roping** hanging down ropelike   **49 gimmaled**
jointed   **51 executors** those who will dispose of what remains behind
54 battle army

CONSTABLE

    They have said their prayers, and they stay for death. 56

DAUPHIN

    Shall we go send them dinners and fresh suits,

    And give their fasting horses provender, 58

    And after fight with them?

CONSTABLE

    I stay but for my guard. On to the field! 60

    I will the banner from a trumpet take 61

    And use it for my haste. Come, come, away!

    The sun is high, and we outwear the day.   *Exeunt.* 63

❖

4.3   *Enter Gloucester, Bedford, Exeter, Erpingham,*
        with all his host, Salisbury, and Westmorland.

GLOUCESTER Where is the King?

BEDFORD

    The King himself is rode to view their battle. 2

WESTMORLAND

    Of fighting men they have full threescore thousand.

EXETER

    There's five to one. Besides, they are all fresh.

SALISBURY

    God's arm strike with us! 'Tis a fearful odds.

    God b' wi' you, princes all; I'll to my charge. 6

    If we no more meet till we meet in heaven,

    Then joyfully, my noble lord of Bedford,

    My dear lord Gloucester, and my good lord Exeter,

    And my kind kinsman, warriors all, adieu! 10

BEDFORD

    Farewell, good Salisbury, and good luck go with thee!

EXETER

    Farewell, kind lord. Fight valiantly today!

    And yet I do thee wrong to mind thee of it, 13

---

56 stay for await **58 provender** fodder **60 guard** (including a
standard-bearer) **61 trumpet** trumpeter **63 outwear** waste

4.3. Location: The English camp.
2 battle army **6 charge** post, command **10 kinsman** i.e., Westmorland,
whose son had married Salisbury's daughter **13 mind** remind

For thou art framed of the firm truth of valor.   14
                              [*Exit Salisbury.*]

BEDFORD
He is as full of valor as of kindness,
Princely in both.

    Enter the King.

WESTMORLAND   O, that we now had here
But one ten thousand of those men in England
That do no work today!
KING   What's he that wishes so?   18
My cousin Westmorland? No, my fair cousin.
If we are marked to die, we are enough   20
To do our country loss; and if to live,   21
The fewer men, the greater share of honor.
God's will, I pray thee, wish not one man more.
By Jove, I am not covetous for gold,
Nor care I who doth feed upon my cost;   25
It yearns me not if men my garments wear;   26
Such outward things dwell not in my desires.
But if it be a sin to covet honor
I am the most offending soul alive.
No, faith, my coz, wish not a man from England.   30
God's peace, I would not lose so great an honor
As one man more, methinks, would share from me   32
For the best hope I have. O, do not wish one more!
Rather proclaim it, Westmorland, through my host   34
That he which hath no stomach to this fight,   35
Let him depart; his passport shall be made
And crowns for convoy put into his purse.   37
We would not die in that man's company
That fears his fellowship to die with us.   39
This day is called the Feast of Crispian.   40
He that outlives this day and comes safe home

14 **framed** made, built   18 **What's** who is   20–21 **enough . . . loss**
enough loss for our country to suffer   25 **upon my cost** at my expense   26 **yearns** grieves   30 **coz** cousin, kinsman   32 **share from me**
take from me as his share   34 **host** army   35 **stomach to** appetite for
37 **crowns for convoy** travel money   39 **That . . . us** that is afraid to risk
his life in my company   40 **Feast of Crispian** Saint Crispin's Day,
October 25. (Cripinus and Crispianus were martyrs who fled from Rome
in the third century; according to legend they disguised themselves as
shoemakers, and afterward became the patron saints of that craft.)

Will stand a-tiptoe when this day is named
And rouse him at the name of Crispian.
He that shall see this day and live old age   44
Will yearly on the vigil feast his neighbors   45
And say, "Tomorrow is Saint Crispian."
Then will he strip his sleeve and show his scars,
And say, "These wounds I had on Crispin's Day."
Old men forget; yet all shall be forgot,   49
But he'll remember with advantages   50
What feats he did that day. Then shall our names,
Familiar in his mouth as household words—
Harry the King, Bedford and Exeter,
Warwick and Talbot, Salisbury and Gloucester—
Be in their flowing cups freshly remembered.   55
This story shall the good man teach his son;
And Crispin Crispian shall ne'er go by,
From this day to the ending of the world,
But we in it shall be rememberèd—
We few, we happy few, we band of brothers.
For he today that sheds his blood with me
Shall be my brother; be he ne'er so vile,   62
This day shall gentle his condition.   63
And gentlemen in England now abed
Shall think themselves accursed they were not here,
And hold their manhoods cheap whiles any speaks
That fought with us upon Saint Crispin's Day.

  Enter Salisbury.

SALISBURY
  My sovereign lord, bestow yourself with speed.   68
  The French are bravely in their battles set   69
  And will with all expedience charge on us.   70
KING
  All things are ready, if our minds be so.
WESTMORLAND
  Perish the man whose mind is backward now!   72

44 live live to see   **45 vigil** evening before a feast day   **49 yet** in time
50 advantages additions of his own   **55 flowing** overflowing   **62 vile**
lowly   **63 gentle his condition** raise him to the rank of gentleman
68 bestow yourself take up your battle position   **69 bravely . . . set** finely
arrayed in their battalions   **70 expedience** speed   **72 backward** reluctant

KING
  Thou dost not wish more help from England, coz?
WESTMORLAND
  God's will, my liege, would you and I alone,
  Without more help, could fight this royal battle!
KING
  Why, now thou hast unwished five thousand men,
  Which likes me better than to wish us one.—   77
  You know your places. God be with you all!

    Tucket. Enter Montjoy.

MONTJOY
  Once more I come to know of thee, King Harry,
  If for thy ransom thou wilt now compound   80
  Before thy most assurèd overthrow;
  For certainly thou art so near the gulf   82
  Thou needs must be englutted. Besides, in mercy   83
  The Constable desires thee thou wilt mind   84
  Thy followers of repentance, that their souls
  May make a peaceful and a sweet retire   86
  From off these fields where, wretches, their poor bodies
  Must lie and fester.
KING   Who hath sent thee now?
MONTJOY   The Constable of France.
KING
  I pray thee, bear my former answer back:
  Bid them achieve me, and then sell my bones.   91
  Good God, why should they mock poor fellows thus?
  The man that once did sell the lion's skin
  While the beast lived was killed with hunting him.
  A many of our bodies shall no doubt   95
  Find native graves, upon the which, I trust,   96
  Shall witness live in brass of this day's work.
  And those that leave their valiant bones in France,
  Dying like men, though buried in your dunghills,
  They shall be famed; for there the sun shall greet them
  And draw their honors reeking up to heaven,   101

77 likes pleases   **80 compound** make terms   **82 gulf** whirlpool   **83 englutted** swallowed up   **84 mind** remind   **86 retire** retreat   **91 achieve**
capture   **95 A many** many. (The phrase is an exact parallel to "a few.")
96 native in their own land (i.e., England)   **101 reeking** (1) breathing
(2) smelling

Leaving their earthly parts to choke your clime,
The smell whereof shall breed a plague in France.
Mark then abounding valor in our English,   104
That, being dead, like to the bullets crazing   105
Break out into a second course of mischief,
Killing in relapse of mortality.   107
Let me speak proudly. Tell the Constable
We are but warriors for the working day.   109
Our gayness and our gilt are all besmirched
With rainy marching in the painful field.
There's not a piece of feather in our host—
Good argument, I hope, we will not fly—
And time hath worn us into slovenry.
But, by the Mass, our hearts are in the trim!
And my poor soldiers tell me, yet ere night
They'll be in fresher robes, or they will pluck   117
The gay new coats o'er the French soldiers' heads
And turn them out of service. If they do this—   119
As, if God please, they shall—my ransom then
Will soon be levied. Herald, save thou thy labor.   121
Come thou no more for ransom, gentle herald.   122
They shall have none, I swear, but these my joints,
Which if they have as I will leave 'em them,
Shall yield them little, tell the Constable.

MONTJOY
I shall, King Harry. And so fare thee well.
Thou never shalt hear herald any more.   *Exit.*

KING
I fear thou wilt once more come again for a ransom.

    Enter York [and kneels].

YORK
My lord, most humbly on my knee I beg
The leading of the vaward.   130

104 abounding overflowing, abundant   **105 crazing** shattering, with a
suggestion also of *grazing*, ricocheting   **107 Killing . . . mortality** killing
(their foes) as they (the English) fall back (decompose) into their elements; also, like the bullet, with a deadly ricochet   **109 for the working
day** i.e., to do serious work, not take a holiday   **117 in fresher robes** i.e.,
in heavenly garb. (Or perhaps the phrase *or they will* means "even if
they have to.")   **119 turn . . . service** i.e., send them away stripped of
their finery, like dismissed servants stripped of their livery   **121 levied**
collected   **122 gentle** noble   **130 vaward** vanguard

KING
　　Take it, brave York. Now, soldiers, march away.
　　And how thou pleasest, God, dispose the day!
　　　　　　　　　　　　　　　　　　　　　　　Exeunt.

❖

4.4　　*Alarum. Excursions. Enter Pistol, French
　　　　Soldier, [and] Boy.*

PISTOL　Yield, cur!
FRENCH SOLDIER　*Je pense que vous êtes le gentilhomme*　2
　　de bonne qualité.　　　　　　　　　　　　　　　　　　3
PISTOL
　　Qualtitie calmie custure me!　　　　　　　　　　　4
　　Art thou a gentleman? What is thy name? Discuss.　5
FRENCH SOLDIER　*O Seigneur Dieu!*　　　　　　　　6
PISTOL
　　O, Signieur Dew should be a gentleman.
　　Perpend my words, O Signieur Dew, and mark:　　8
　　O Signieur Dew, thou diest on point of fox,　　　9
　　Except, O signieur, thou do give to me　　　　　10
　　Egregious ransom. [*He threatens him with his sword.*]　11
FRENCH SOLDIER　*O, prenez miséricorde! Ayez pitié de*　12
　　moi!　　　　　　　　　　　　　　　　　　　　　13
PISTOL
　　"Moy" shall not serve. I will have forty moys,　　14
　　Or I will fetch thy rim out at thy throat　　　　15
　　In drops of crimson blood.
FRENCH SOLDIER　*Est-il impossible d'échapper la force*　17
　　de ton bras?　　　　　　　　　　　　　　　　　18

4.4. Location: The field of battle.
s.d. Excursions sorties　**2–3 Je . . . qualité** I think that you are a gentleman of high rank　**4 calmie custure me** (These words are perhaps
derived from the refrain of a popular song, supposed to be Irish, "Calen
o custure me.")　**5 Discuss** speak　**6 O Seigneur Dieu** O Lord God
8 Perpend attend to, consider　**9 fox** sword　**10 Except** unless
11 Egregious huge　**12–13 O . . . moi** Oh, have mercy! Take pity on
me!　**14 Moy** (Pistol, not understanding, takes *moi* for the name of a
coin, or a sum of money.)　**15 rim** midriff, diaphragm　**17–18 Est-il . . .
bras** is it impossible to escape the strength of your arm. (But Pistol
takes *bras*, arm, for *brass*.)

PISTOL   Brass, cur?
  Thou damnèd and luxurious mountain goat,   20
  Offer'st me brass?
FRENCH SOLDIER   *O, pardonnez-moi!*
PISTOL
  Sayst thou me so? Is that a ton of moys?   23
  Come hither, boy. Ask me this slave in French
  What is his name.
BOY   *Écoutez: comment êtes-vous appelé?*   26
FRENCH SOLDIER   *Monsieur le Fer.*
BOY   He says his name is Master Fer.
PISTOL   Master Fer? I'll fer him, and firk him, and ferret 29
  him. Discuss the same in French unto him.
BOY   I do not know the French for fer, and ferret, and
  firk.
PISTOL
  Bid him prepare, for I will cut his throat.
FRENCH SOLDIER   *Que dit-il, monsieur?*   34
BOY   *Il me commande à vous dire que vous faites vous*   35
  prêt; car ce soldat ici est disposé tout à cette heure de   36
  couper votre gorge.   37
PISTOL
  Owy, cuppele gorge, permafoy,   38
  Peasant, unless thou give me crowns, brave crowns,
  Or mangled shalt thou be by this my sword.
FRENCH SOLDIER   *O, je vous supplie, pour l'amour de*   41
  Dieu, me pardonner! Je suis le gentilhomme de bonne   42
  maison. Gardez ma vie, et je vous donnerai deux cents   43
  écus.   44
PISTOL   What are his words?
BOY   He prays you to save his life. He is a gentleman of
  a good house, and for his ransom he will give you two   47
  hundred crowns.

---

20 luxurious lecherous   **23 a ton of moys** (This is what Pistol phoneti-
cally makes out of *pardonnez-moi*.)   **26 Écoutez . . . appelé** listen: what
is your name   **29 firk** trounce.   **ferret** worry (like a ferret)   **34–37 Que
. . . gorge** What does he say, sir? BOY He bids me tell you that you must
prepare yourself, because this soldier intends to cut your throat immediately   **38 Owy** i.e., *oui*, yes.   **permafoy** *per ma foi*, by my faith
41–44 O . . . écus Oh, I pray you, for the love of God, to pardon me. I am
a gentleman of a good house; preserve my life, and I shall give you two
hundred crowns   **47 house** family

PISTOL
   Tell him my fury shall abate, and I
   The crowns will take.
FRENCH SOLDIER   *Petit monsieur, que dit-il?*   51
BOY   *Encore qu'il est contre son jurement de pardonner*   52
   aucun prisonnier, néanmoins, pour les écus que vous   53
   l'avez promis, il est content à vous donner la liberté,   54
   le franchisement.   55
FRENCH SOLDIER   [*Kneeling*]   *Sur mes genoux je vous*   56
   donne mille remercîments; et je m'estime heureux que   57
   j'ai tombé entre les mains d'un chevalier, je pense,   58
   le plus brave, vaillant, et très-distingué seigneur   59
   d'Angleterre.   60
PISTOL   Expound unto me, boy.
BOY   He gives you, upon his knees, a thousand thanks,
   and he esteems himself happy that he hath fallen into
   the hands of one, as he thinks, the most brave, valor-
   ous, and thrice-worthy seigneur of England.
PISTOL
   As I suck blood, I will some mercy show.
   Follow me!
BOY   *Suivez-vous le grand capitaine.* [*Exeunt Pistol and*   68
   French Soldier.] I did never know so full a voice issue
   from so empty a heart! But the saying is true, "The
   empty vessel makes the greatest sound." Bardolph and
   Nym had ten times more valor than this roaring devil   72
   i' th' old play, that everyone may pare his nails with
   a wooden dagger, and they are both hanged; and so
   would this be, if he durst steal anything adventur-
   ously. I must stay with the lackeys, with the luggage
   of our camp. The French might have a good prey of   77
   us, if he knew of it, for there is none to guard it but
   boys.   *Exit.*

51–55 Petit . . . franchisement What does he say, little sir? BOY Although
it is against his oath to pardon any prisoner, nevertheless, for the sake
of the crowns you have promised, he is willing to give you your liberty,
your freedom   **56–60 Sur . . . d'Angleterre** On my knees I give you a
thousand thanks; and I consider myself happy that I have fallen into the
hands of a knight, as I think, the bravest, most valiant, and very distin-
guished gentleman in England   **68 Suivez-vous . . . capitaine** follow the
great captain   **72 roaring devil** i.e., the devil in the morality play, a
comic figure paired with the Vice who traditionally had a wooden
dagger   **77 a good prey** i.e., easy pickings

4.5   *Enter Constable, Orleans, Bourbon, Dauphin,*
         and Rambures.

CONSTABLE   *O diable!*   1
ORLEANS   *O Seigneur! Le jour est perdu, tout est perdu!*   2
DAUPHIN
  Mort de ma vie! All is confounded, all.   3
  Reproach and everlasting shame
  Sits mocking in our plumes.   *A short alarum.*
  O méchante fortune! Do not run away.   6
CONSTABLE   Why, all our ranks are broke.
DAUPHIN
  O perdurable shame! Let's stab ourselves.   8
  Be these the wretches that we played at dice for?
ORLEANS
  Is this the king we sent to for his ransom?
BOURBON
  Shame and eternal shame, nothing but shame!
  Let us die! In once more! Back again!
  And he that will not follow Bourbon now,
  Let him go hence, and with his cap in hand,
  Like a base pander, hold the chamber door
  Whilst by a slave, no gentler than my dog,   16
  His fairest daughter is contaminated.
CONSTABLE
  Disorder, that hath spoiled us, friend us now!   18
  Let us on heaps go offer up our lives.   19
ORLEANS
  We are enough yet living in the field
  To smother up the English in our throngs,
  If any order might be thought upon.
BOURBON
  The devil take order now! I'll to the throng.
  Let life be short, else shame will be too long.

                                        Exeunt.

4.5. Location: The field of battle still.
1 O diable O the devil   **2 O . . . perdu** O Lord, the day is lost, all is
lost   **3 Mort de ma vie** death of my life, i.e., may my life end.   **confounded** lost   **6 O méchante fortune** O malicious fortune   **8 perdurable**
everlasting   **16 gentler** (1) more nobly born (2) tenderer   **18 friend**
befriend   **19 on** in

4.6 *Alarum. Enter the King and his train, [Exeter, and others,] with prisoners.*

KING
Well have we done, thrice valiant countrymen!
But all's not done; yet keep the French the field.

EXETER
The Duke of York commends him to Your Majesty.

KING
Lives he, good uncle? Thrice within this hour
I saw him down, thrice up again and fighting.
From helmet to the spur all blood he was.

EXETER
In which array, brave soldier, doth he lie,
Larding the plain; and by his bloody side,   8
Yokefellow to his honor-owing wounds,   9
The noble Earl of Suffolk also lies.
Suffolk first died; and York, all haggled over,   11
Comes to him where in gore he lay insteeped   12
And takes him by the beard, kisses the gashes
That bloodily did yawn upon his face.   14
He cries aloud, "Tarry, my cousin Suffolk!
My soul shall thine keep company to heaven;
Tarry, sweet soul, for mine, then fly abreast,
As in this glorious and well-foughten field
We kept together in our chivalry!"
Upon these words I came and cheered him up.
He smiled me in the face, raught me his hand,   21
And, with a feeble grip, says, "Dear my lord,
Commend my service to my sovereign."
So did he turn, and over Suffolk's neck
He threw his wounded arm, and kissed his lips,
And so espoused to death, with blood he sealed
A testament of noble-ending love.
The pretty and sweet manner of it forced
Those waters from me which I would have stopped;   29

4.6. Location: The field of battle still.
8 Larding fattening, enriching (with his blood)   **9 honor-owing** honor-owning, honorable   **11 haggled over** mangled, hacked   **12 insteeped** immersed   **14 yawn** gape   **21 me in the** i.e., in my.   **raught** reached   **29 Those waters** i.e., tears

But I had not so much of man in me,
And all my mother came into mine eyes   31
And gave me up to tears.
KING   I blame you not;
For, hearing this, I must perforce compound   33
With mistful eyes, or they will issue too.   *Alarum.* 34
But, hark, what new alarum is this same?
The French have reinforced their scattered men.
Then every soldier kill his prisoners!   37
Give the word through.   *Exit [with others].*

4.7   *Enter Fluellen and Gower.*

FLUELLEN Kill the poys and the luggage! 'Tis expressly 1
against the law of arms. 'Tis as arrant a piece of knav-
ery, mark you now, as can be offert; in your conscience, now, is it not?
GOWER 'Tis certain there's not a boy left alive; and the
cowardly rascals that ran from the battle ha' done this
slaughter. Besides, they have burned and carried away
all that was in the King's tent, wherefore the King
most worthily hath caused every soldier to cut his
prisoner's throat. O, 'tis a gallant king!
FLUELLEN Ay, he was porn at Monmouth, Captain 11
Gower. What call you the town's name where Alexander the Pig was born?
GOWER Alexander the Great.
FLUELLEN Why, I pray you, is not "pig" great? The pig,
or the great, or the mighty, or the huge, or the mag-

---

31 my mother i.e., the tenderer part of me **33 perforce** necessarily.
compound come to terms **34 issue** i.e., issue forth tears **37 kill his
prisoners** (This follows Holinshed, who says that Henry, alarmed by the
outcry of the lackeys and boys of the camp, feared a new attack and
ordered the prisoners killed as a means of precaution. Gower, 4.7.9–10,
attributes the King's action to revenge.)

4.7. Location: The field of battle still.
1 luggage i.e., lackeys guarding the luggage **11 Monmouth** (i.e., in
Wales)

nanimous, are all one reckonings, save the phrase is a 17
little variations.

GOWER I think Alexander the Great was born in Macedon. His father was called Philip of Macedon, as I
take it.

FLUELLEN I think it is in Macedon where Alexander is
porn. I tell you, Captain, if you look in the maps of the
'orld, I warrant you sall find, in the comparisons between Macedon and Monmouth, that the situations,
look you, is both alike. There is a river in Macedon,
and there is also moreover a river at Monmouth. It is
called Wye at Monmouth, but it is out of my prains
what is the name of the other river; but 'tis all one, 'tis
alike as my fingers is to my fingers, and there is salm-
ons in both. If you mark Alexander's life well, Harry
of Monmouth's life is come after it indifferent well, for 32
there is figures in all things. Alexander, God knows, 33
and you know, in his rages, and his furies, and his
wraths, and his cholers, and his moods, and his dis-
pleasures, and his indignations, and also being a little
intoxicates in his prains, did, in his ales and his an- 37
gers, look you, kill his best friend, Cleitus. 38

GOWER Our King is not like him in that. He never killed
any of his friends.

FLUELLEN It is not well done, mark you now, to take the
tales out of my mouth ere it is made and finished. I
speak but in the figures and comparisons of it. As Alexander killed his friend Cleitus, being in his ales and
his cups, so also Harry Monmouth, being in his right
wits and his good judgments, turned away the fat
knight with the great-belly doublet. He was full of 47
jests, and gipes, and knaveries, and mocks. I have for- 48
got his name.

GOWER Sir John Falstaff.

17 **reckonings** judgment, evaluation. **is** i.e., has undergone **32 is . . .
well** resembles it fairly well **33 figures** comparisons, similes **37 in his
ales** i.e., under the influence of ale **38 Cleitus** a general and close
associate of Alexander, whom Alexander killed in a drinking bout
47 great-belly doublet a man's close-fitting jacket in which the lower
part was stuffed out with bombast or padding **48 gipes** jibes, jokes

FLUELLEN   That is he. I'll tell you there is good men porn
   at Monmouth.
GOWER   Here comes His Majesty.

Alarum. Enter King Harry, [Warwick, Gloucester,
Exeter, and others,] and Bourbon with [other]
prisoners. Flourish.

KING
   I was not angry since I came to France
   Until this instant. Take a trumpet, herald;   55
   Ride thou unto the horsemen on yond hill.
   If they will fight with us, bid them come down,
   Or void the field. They do offend our sight.   58
   If they'll do neither, we will come to them,
   And make them skirr away as swift as stones   60
   Enforcèd from the old Assyrian slings.   61
   Besides, we'll cut the throats of those we have,
   And not a man of them that we shall take
   Shall taste our mercy. Go and tell them so.

   Enter Montjoy.

EXETER
   Here comes the herald of the French, my liege.
GLOUCESTER
   His eyes are humbler than they used to be.
KING
   How now, what means this, herald? Know'st thou not
   That I have fined these bones of mine for ransom?   68
   Com'st thou again for ransom?
MONTJOY   No, great King.
   I come to thee for charitable license,
   That we may wander o'er this bloody field
   To book our dead and then to bury them,   72
   To sort our nobles from our common men.
   For many of our princes—woe the while!—
   Lie drowned and soaked in mercenary blood;   75
   So do our vulgar drench their peasant limbs   76

55 **trumpet** trumpeter   58 **void** leave   60 **skirr** scurry   61 **Enforcèd**
discharged   68 **fined . . . ransom** i.e., agreed to pay as a fine or ransom
only these bones of mine and no more   72 **book** record   75 **mer-**
cenary i.e., of common soldiers, who fought for pay   76 **vulgar**
commoners

In blood of princes; and the wounded steeds
Fret fetlock-deep in gore and with wild rage
Yerk out their armèd heels at their dead masters,   79
Killing them twice. O, give us leave, great King,
To view the field in safety, and dispose
Of their dead bodies!

KING   I tell thee truly, herald,
I know not if the day be ours or no,
For yet a many of your horsemen peer   84
And gallop o'er the field.

MONTJOY   The day is yours.

KING
Praised be God, and not our strength, for it!
What is this castle called that stands hard by?

MONTJOY   They call it Agincourt.

KING
Then call we this the field of Agincourt,
Fought on the day of Crispin Crispianus.

FLUELLEN   Your grandfather of famous memory, an 't   91
please Your Majesty, and your great-uncle Edward the
Plack Prince of Wales, as I have read in the chronicles,
fought a most prave pattle here in France.

KING   They did, Fluellen.

FLUELLEN   Your Majesty says very true. If Your Majesties
is remembered of it, the Welshmen did good service in
a garden where leeks did grow, wearing leeks in their
Monmouth caps, which, Your Majesty know, to this   99
hour is an honorable badge of the service; and I do
believe Your Majesty takes no scorn to wear the leek
upon Saint Tavy's Day.

KING
I wear it for a memorable honor,
For I am Welsh, you know, good countryman.

FLUELLEN   All the water in Wye cannot wash Your Majesty's Welsh plood out of your pody, I can tell you
that. God pless it and preserve it, as long as it pleases
His Grace, and His Majesty too!

KING   Thanks, good my countryman.

---

79 Yerk kick   **84 peer** (1) look about anxiously (2) appear   **91 grandfather** i.e., great-grandfather, Edward III.   **an 't** if it   **99 Monmouth
caps** round and rimless caps with a tapering crown, commonly worn
by the Welsh

FLUELLEN   By Jeshu, I am Your Majesty's countryman, I
care not who know it. I will confess it to all the 'orld.
I need not to be ashamed of Your Majesty, praised be
God, so long as Your Majesty is an honest man.

KING
God keep me so!

Enter Williams [with a glove in his cap].

                    Our heralds go with him.
Bring me just notice of the numbers dead   115
On both our parts.

                    [Exeunt Heralds and Gower with Montjoy.]
                    Call yonder fellow hither.

EXETER   Soldier, you must come to the King.

KING   Soldier, why wear'st thou that glove in thy cap?

WILLIAMS   An 't please Your Majesty, 'tis the gage of one
that I should fight withal, if he be alive.

KING   An Englishman?

WILLIAMS   An 't please Your Majesty, a rascal that swag-
gered with me last night, who, if 'a live and ever dare
to challenge this glove, I have sworn to take him a box
o' th' ear; or if I can see my glove in his cap, which he
swore as he was a soldier he would wear if 'a lived, I
will strike it out soundly.

KING   What think you, Captain Fluellen, is it fit this soldier keep his oath?

FLUELLEN   He is a craven and a villain else, an 't please   130
Your Majesty, in my conscience.

KING   It may be his enemy is a gentleman of great sort,   132
quite from the answer of his degree.   133

FLUELLEN   Though he be as good a gentleman as the
devil is, as Lucifer and Beelzebub himself, it is necessary, look Your Grace, that he keep his vow and his
oath. If he be perjured, see you now, his reputation is
as arrant a villain and a Jack-sauce as ever his black   138
shoe trod upon God's ground and His earth, in my
conscience, la!

KING   Then keep thy vow, sirrah, when thou meet'st the
fellow.

115 just exact   **130 craven** coward   **132 sort** rank   **133 quite . . . degree**
i.e., too high in rank to answer the challenge of one so low   **138 Jack-
sauce** saucy knave

WILLIAMS   So I will, my liege, as I live.

KING   Who serv'st thou under?

WILLIAMS   Under Captain Gower, my liege.

FLUELLEN   Gower is a good captain, and is good knowl-
edge and literatured in the wars.   147

KING   Call him hither to me, soldier.

WILLIAMS   I will, my liege.   *Exit.*

KING   Here, Fluellen, wear thou this favor for me and
stick it in thy cap. [*He gives Fluellen Williams's glove.*]
When Alençon and myself were down together, I
plucked this glove from his helm. If any man challenge   153
this, he is a friend to Alençon and an enemy to our
person. If thou encounter any such, apprehend him,
an thou dost me love.   156

FLUELLEN [*Putting the glove in his cap*]   Your Grace doo's   157
me as great honors as can be desired in the hearts of
his subjects. I would fain see the man that has but   159
two legs that shall find himself aggriefed at this glove,
that is all. But I would fain see it once, an 't please God   161
of his grace that I might see.

KING   Know'st thou Gower?

FLUELLEN   He is my dear friend, an 't please you.

KING   Pray thee, go seek him and bring him to my tent.

FLUELLEN   I will fetch him.   *Exit.*

KING
My lord of Warwick, and my brother Gloucester,
Follow Fluellen closely at the heels.
The glove which I have given him for a favor
May haply purchase him a box o' th' ear.   170
It is the soldier's; I by bargain should
Wear it myself. Follow, good cousin Warwick.
If that the soldier strike him, as I judge
By his blunt bearing he will keep his word,
Some sudden mischief may arise of it;
For I do know Fluellen valiant
And touched with choler, hot as gunpowder,   177
And quickly will return an injury.   178

147 **literatured** well read   153 **helm** helmet   156 **an** if   157 **doo's**
does   159 **fain** willingly   161 **an 't** if it (also in l. 164)   170 **haply**
perhaps   177 **touched with choler** hot-tempered   178 **return** repay.
injury insult

Follow, and see there be no harm between them.
Go you with me, uncle of Exeter. *Exeunt [separately]*.

✣

4.8   *Enter Gower and Williams.*

WILLIAMS   I warrant it is to knight you, Captain.

　　Enter Fluellen.

FLUELLEN   God's will and his pleasure, Captain, I beseech you now, come apace to the King. There is more
good toward you, peradventure, than is in your knowl- 4
edge to dream of.

WILLIAMS   Sir, know you this glove?

FLUELLEN   Know the glove? I know the glove is a glove.

WILLIAMS   I know this, and thus I challenge it.

　　　　　　　　　　　　　　　　　　Strikes him.

FLUELLEN   'Sblood, an arrant traitor as any 's in the uni- 9
versal world, or in France, or in England!

GOWER [*To Williams*]   How now, sir? You villain!

WILLIAMS   Do you think I'll be forsworn?

FLUELLEN   Stand away, Captain Gower. I will give treason his payment into plows, I warrant you.   14

WILLIAMS   I am no traitor.

FLUELLEN   That's a lie in thy throat. I charge you in His 16
Majesty's name, apprehend him. He's a friend of the
Duke Alençon's.

　　Enter Warwick and Gloucester.

WARWICK   How now, how now, what's the matter?

FLUELLEN   My lord of Warwick, here is—praised be
God for it!—a most contagious treason come to light, 21
look you, as you shall desire in a summer's day.—
Here is His Majesty.

4.8. Location: The English camp.
4 peradventure by chance **9 'Sblood** by His (Christ's) blood **14 his**
its. **into plows** in blows **16 lie in thy throat** i.e., inexcusable lie
21 contagious noxious

Enter King [Henry] and Exeter.

KING   How now, what's the matter?

FLUELLEN   My liege, here is a villain and a traitor that,
look Your Grace, has struck the glove which Your Majesty is take out of the helmet of Alençon.

WILLIAMS   My liege, this was my glove; here is the fellow of it. [*Showing his other glove.*] And he that I gave it
to in change promised to wear it in his cap. I promised 30
to strike him if he did. I met this man with my glove
in his cap, and I have been as good as my word.

FLUELLEN   Your Majesty hear now, saving Your Majesty's manhood, what an arrant, rascally, beggarly,
lousy knave it is. I hope Your Majesty is pear me tes- 35
timony and witness, and will avouchment, that this is 36
the glove of Alençon that Your Majesty is give me, in
your conscience, now.

KING   Give me thy glove, soldier. Look, here is the fel-
low of it.   [*He shows his other glove.*]
'Twas I indeed thou promisèdst to strike,
And thou hast given me most bitter terms.   42

FLUELLEN   An 't please Your Majesty, let his neck answer 43
for it, if there is any martial law in the world.

KING
How canst thou make me satisfaction?

WILLIAMS   All offenses, my lord, come from the heart.
Never came any from mine that might offend Your
Majesty.

KING   It was ourself thou didst abuse.

WILLIAMS   Your Majesty came not like yourself. You appeared to me but as a common man—witness the
night, your garments, your lowliness. And what Your 52
Highness suffered under that shape, I beseech you take
it for your own fault and not mine; for had you been
as I took you for, I made no offense. Therefore I beseech Your Highness pardon me.

KING
Here, uncle Exeter, fill this glove with crowns,
And give it to this fellow. Keep it, fellow,

---

30 change exchange   **35 is pear** will bear   **36 avouchment** avouch
42 terms words   **43 An 't** if it (also in l. 117)   **52 lowliness** humble mien

And wear it for an honor in thy cap
Till I do challenge it. Give him the crowns.
        [*Exeter gives the glove and gold to Williams.*]
And Captain, you must needs be friends with him.

FLUELLEN   By this day and this light, the fellow has mettle enough in his belly. Hold, there is twelvepence for
you. [*He offers a coin.*] And I pray you to serve God, and
keep you out of prawls, and prabbles, and quarrels,   65
and dissensions, and I warrant you it is the better for
you.

WILLIAMS   I will none of your money.

FLUELLEN   It is with a good will. I can tell you, it will
serve you to mend your shoes. Come, wherefore
should you be so pashful? Your shoes is not so good.
'Tis a good silling, I warrant you, or I will change it.

        Enter [an English] Herald.

KING   Now, herald, are the dead numbered?

HERALD [*Giving a paper*]
Here is the number of the slaughtered French.

KING
What prisoners of good sort are taken, uncle?   75

EXETER
Charles Duke of Orleans, nephew to the King;   76
John Duke of Bourbon, and Lord Boucicault;
Of other lords and barons, knights and squires,
Full fifteen hundred, besides common men.

KING
This note doth tell me of ten thousand French
That in the field lie slain. Of princes, in this number,
And nobles bearing banners, there lie dead   82
One hundred twenty-six; added to these,
Of knights, esquires, and gallant gentlemen,
Eight thousand and four hundred, of the which
Five hundred were but yesterday dubbed knights.
So that in these ten thousand they have lost
There are but sixteen hundred mercenaries;
The rest are princes, barons, lords, knights, squires,

---

65 prabbles i.e., brabbles, scuffles   **75 good sort** high rank
76–112 Charles . . . thine (The catalogue of the captured and slain is
from Holinshed.)   **82 bearing banners** i.e., with coats of arms

And gentlemen of blood and quality.
The names of those their nobles that lie dead:
Charles Delabreth, High Constable of France;
Jaques of Chatillion, Admiral of France;
The Master of the Crossbows, Lord Rambures;
Great-Master of France, the brave Sir Guichard Dau-
   phin;   95
John, Duke of Alençon; Anthony Duke of Brabant,
The brother to the Duke of Burgundy;
And Edward, Duke of Bar; of lusty earls,   98
Grandpré and Roussi, Faulconbridge and Foix,
Beaumont and Marle, Vaudemont and Lestrelles.
Here was a royal fellowship of death!
Where is the number of our English dead?
                    [*He is given another paper.*]
Edward the Duke of York, the Earl of Suffolk,
Sir Richard Keighley, Davy Gam, esquire;
None else of name, and of all other men   105
But five-and-twenty. O God, thy arm was here!
And not to us, but to thy arm alone,
Ascribe we all! When, without stratagem,
But in plain shock and even play of battle,   109
Was ever known so great and little loss
On one part and on th' other? Take it, God,
For it is none but thine!
EXETER   'Tis wonderful.
KING
Come, go we in procession to the village.
And be it death proclaimèd through our host
To boast of this or take that praise from God
Which is his only.
FLUELLEN   Is it not lawful, an 't please Your Majesty, to
tell how many is killed?
KING
Yes, Captain, but with this acknowledgment,
That God fought for us.
FLUELLEN   Yes, in my conscience, he did us great good.
KING   Do we all holy rites.

---

95 Great-Master grandmaster, i.e., the chief officer of the royal household   **98 lusty** vigorous   **105 name** rank, importance   **109 shock**
confrontation.   **even** equal

Let there be sung *Non nobis* and *Te Deum*,   123
The dead with charity enclosed in clay;
And then to Calais, and to England then,
Where ne'er from France arrived more happy men.   126

                         Exeunt.

✤

123 **Non nobis** i.e., Psalm 115, beginning, "Not unto us, O Lord, not unto us, but unto thy name give glory." **Te Deum** a hymn of thanksgiving, beginning, "We praise thee O God" **126 happy** fortunate

5.0   *Enter Chorus.*

CHORUS

Vouchsafe to those that have not read the story   1
That I may prompt them; and of such as have,
I humbly pray them to admit th' excuse   3
Of time, of numbers, and due course of things,
Which cannot in their huge and proper life
Be here presented. Now we bear the King
Toward Calais. Grant him there. There seen,
Heave him away upon your wingèd thoughts
Athwart the sea. Behold, the English beach
Pales in the flood with men, wives, and boys,   10
Whose shouts and claps outvoice the deep-mouthed sea,
Which like a mighty whiffler 'fore the King   12
Seems to prepare his way. So let him land,
And solemnly see him set on to London.
So swift a pace hath thought that even now
You may imagine him upon Blackheath,   16
Where that his lords desire him to have borne   17
His bruisèd helmet and his bended sword
Before him through the city. He forbids it,
Being free from vainness and self-glorious pride,
Giving full trophy, signal, and ostent   21
Quite from himself to God. But now behold,
In the quick forge and working-house of thought,
How London doth pour out her citizens!
The Mayor and all his brethren in best sort,   25
Like to the senators of th' antique Rome
With the plebeians swarming at their heels,
Go forth and fetch their conquering Caesar in;

5.0. (Between Acts 4 and 5 there is historically an interval of about five
years during which Henry made a second campaign in France that
brought the French to terms in the Treaty of Troyes, with which the
play ends.)
1 Vouchsafe permit it   3 admit th' excuse excuse our handling
10 Pales in hems in, surrounds.   flood sea   12 whiffler an usher head-
ing the procession to clear the way   16 Blackheath open area just
outside London, to the southeast   17 Where that where   21 signal
token (of victory).   ostent external show   25 sort array

As by a lower but loving likelihood,   29
Were now the General of our gracious Empress,   30
As in good time he may, from Ireland coming,
Bringing rebellion broachèd on his sword,   32
How many would the peaceful city quit
To welcome him! Much more, and much more cause,   34
Did they this Harry. Now in London place him;
As yet the lamentation of the French   36
Invites the King of England's stay at home;   37
The Emperor's coming in behalf of France,   38
To order peace between them . . . and omit   39
All the occurrences, whatever chanced,
Till Harry's back-return again to France.   41
There must we bring him; and myself have played
The interim, by remembering you 'tis past.   43
Then brook abridgment, and your eyes advance,   44
After your thoughts, straight back again to France.

                                                            Exit.

5.1   *Enter Fluellen [with a leek in his cap, and a*
           cudgel], and Gower.

GOWER   Nay, that's right. But why wear you your leek
    today? Saint Davy's Day is past.
FLUELLEN   There is occasions and causes why and
    wherefore in all things. I will tell you asse my friend,   4

29–34 As . . . him (Seemingly an allusion to the Earl of Essex, who left
London on his Irish expedition on March 27, 1599, in an attempt to put
down Tyrone's rebellion; he returned unsuccessful and under a cloud on
September 28 of the same year. These lines, therefore, were probably
written between the dates mentioned.)   29 a . . . likelihood a less exalted
comparison but one that shows much love   30 Empress i.e., Elizabeth
32 broachèd transfixed, spitted   36–37 As . . . home i.e., the French are so
dejected that Henry can stay in England without fear of loss in France
38 Emperor's coming (The Holy Roman Emperor, Sigismund, came to
England on behalf of France in May 1416.)   39 them . . . and omit (Something appears to be left out here. Possibly it should read, "them, and the
death / O' the Dauphin, leap we over, and omit . . .")   41 Harry's back-
return i.e., Henry's second campaign, commencing in 1417
43 remembering reminding   44 brook tolerate, excuse

5.1. Location: France. The English camp.
4 asse as

Captain Gower. The rascally, scald, beggarly, lousy, 5
pragging knave, Pistol, which you and yourself and all
the world know to be no petter than a fellow, look you
now, of no merits, he is come to me and prings me
pread and salt yesterday, look you, and bid me eat my
leek. It was in a place where I could not breed no con-
tention with him; but I will be so bold as to wear it in
my cap till I see him once again, and then I will tell
him a little piece of my desires.

Enter Pistol.

GOWER   Why, here he comes, swelling like a turkey-
cock.

FLUELLEN   'Tis no matter for his swellings nor his tur-
key-cocks.—God pless you, Aunchient Pistol! You
scurvy, lousy knave, God pless you!

PISTOL
Ha, art thou bedlam? Dost thou thirst, base Trojan,   19
To have me fold up Parca's fatal web?   20
Hence, I am qualmish at the smell of leek.   21

FLUELLEN   I peseech you heartily, scurvy, lousy knave,
at my desires, and my requests, and my petitions, to
eat, look you, this leek. [*He offers the leek.*] Because,
look you, you do not love it, nor your affections and
your appetites and your disgestions doo's not agree
with it, I would desire you to eat it.

PISTOL
Not for Cadwallader and all his goats.   28

FLUELLEN   There is one goat for you. (*Strikes him.*) Will
you be so good, scald knave, as eat it?

PISTOL   Base Trojan, thou shalt die.

FLUELLEN   You say very true, scald knave, when God's
will is. I will desire you to live in the meantime and
eat your victuals. Come, there is sauce for it. [*He strikes
him.*] You called me yesterday mountain squire, but I   35

---

5 scald scurvy   **19 bedlam** crazy.   **Trojan** i.e., rascal   **20 Parca's** (The
Parcae, or Fates, spun, drew out, and cut the thread of destiny.)   **21 qualmish** squeamish, nauseated   **28 Cadwallader** last king of the Welsh.   **goats**
(Pistol makes the customary taunt that the Welsh were goatherds.)
35 mountain squire i.e., a squire owning mountainous, poor land

will make you today a squire of low degree. I pray 36
you, fall to. If you can mock a leek, you can eat a leek.

GOWER Enough, Captain, you have astonished him.   38

FLUELLEN By Jesu, I will make him eat some part of my
leek, or I will peat his pate four days. Bite, I pray you; 40
it is good for your green wound and your ploody cox- 41
comb.   42

PISTOL Must I bite?

FLUELLEN Yes, certainly, and out of doubt and out of
question too, and ambiguities.

PISTOL
By this leek, I will most horribly revenge—
                              [*Fluellen threatens him.*]
I eat and eat—I swear—

FLUELLEN Eat, I pray you. Will you have some more
sauce to your leek? There is not enough leek to
swear by.

PISTOL
Quiet thy cudgel; thou dost see I eat.

FLUELLEN Much good do you, scald knave, heartily.
Nay, pray you, throw none away; the skin is good for
your broken coxcomb. When you take occasions to see
leeks hereafter, I pray you, mock at 'em, that is all.

PISTOL Good.

FLUELLEN Ay, leeks is good. Hold you, there is a groat 57
to heal your pate.   [*He offers a coin.*]

PISTOL Me, a groat?

FLUELLEN Yes, verily, and in truth you shall take it, or
I have another leek in my pocket which you shall eat.

PISTOL
I take thy groat in earnest of revenge.   62

FLUELLEN If I owe you anything, I will pay you in cudgels. You shall be a woodmonger and buy nothing of
me but cudgels. God b' wi' you, and keep you, and heal
your pate.   *Exit.*

PISTOL All hell shall stir for this.

---

36 squire of low degree (Allusion to a popular medieval romance, *The
Squire of Low Degree.* Fluellen threatens to make Pistol into a lowly,
contemptible figure, towered over by a mountain squire.) **38 astonished** dazed, terrified **40 pate** head **41 green** raw **41–42 coxcomb**
fool's cap; here, the scalp **57 groat** fourpenny coin **62 in earnest of** as
a down payment for

GOWER Go, go, you are a counterfeit cowardly knave.
Will you mock at an ancient tradition, begun upon an
honorable respect and worn as a memorable trophy 70
of predeceased valor, and dare not avouch in your 71
deeds any of your words? I have seen you gleeking 72
and galling at this gentleman twice or thrice. You 73
thought because he could not speak English in the
native garb he could not therefore handle an English
cudgel. You find it otherwise; and henceforth let a
Welsh correction teach you a good English condition.
Fare ye well.   *Exit.*

PISTOL
Doth Fortune play the huswife with me now?   79
News have I that my Doll is dead   80
I' th' spital of a malady of France,   81
And there my rendezvous is quite cut off.   82
Old I do wax, and from my weary limbs   83
Honor is cudgeled. Well, bawd I'll turn,
And something lean to cutpurse of quick hand.   85
To England will I steal, and there I'll steal;
And patches will I get unto these cudgeled scars,
And swear I got them in the Gallia wars.   *Exit.* 88

❖

5.2   *Enter, at one door, King Henry, Exeter,*
Bedford, [Gloucester, Clarence,] Warwick,
[Westmorland,] and other lords; at another,
Queen Isabel, the [French] King, the Duke of
Burgundy, [the Princess Katharine, Alice,] and
other French.

KING HENRY
Peace to this meeting, wherefor we are met!
Unto our brother France and to our sister,
Health and fair time of day; joy and good wishes

70 **respect** consideration 71 **predeceased valor** valor of those now dead
72–73 **gleeking and galling** mocking and scoffing 79 **huswife** hussy, fickle
one 80 **Doll** (An error for *Nell;* may indicate an earlier version in which
the speaker of these lines was Falstaff.) 81 **spital** hospital. **malady of
France** veneral disease 82 **rendezvous** refuge 83 **wax** grow 85 **something lean to** incline somewhat to 88 **Gallia** French

5.2. Location: The French court.

To our most fair and princely cousin Katharine;
And, as a branch and member of this royalty,   5
By whom this great assembly is contrived,
We do salute you, Duke of Burgundy;
And princes French, and peers, health to you all!

FRENCH KING
Right joyous are we to behold your face,
Most worthy brother England. Fairly met!
So are you, princes English, every one.

QUEEN ISABEL
So happy be the issue, brother England,   12
Of this good day and of this gracious meeting,
As we are now glad to behold your eyes—
Your eyes, which hitherto have borne in them
Against the French that met them in their bent   16
The fatal balls of murdering basilisks.   17
The venom of such looks, we fairly hope,
Have lost their quality, and that this day
Shall change all griefs and quarrels into love.   20

KING HENRY
To cry amen to that, thus we appear.

QUEEN ISABEL
You English princes all, I do salute you.

BURGUNDY
My duty to you both, on equal love,
Great Kings of France and England! That I have labored
With all my wits, my pains, and strong endeavors
To bring your most imperial Majesties
Unto this bar and royal interview,   27
Your mightiness on both parts best can witness.
Since then my office hath so far prevailed
That, face to face and royal eye to eye,
You have congreeted, let it not disgrace me   31
If I demand, before this royal view,   32
What rub or what impediment there is   33
Why that the naked, poor, and mangled Peace,

---

5 royalty royal family   **12 issue** outcome   **16 in their bent** (1) as they
were directed (2) in their glance   **17 fatal balls** (1) cannon balls (2) eye-
balls.   **basilisks** (1) large cannon (2) monsters supposed to kill with
their gaze   **20 griefs** grievances   **27 bar** court   **31 congreeted** greeted
each other   **32 demand** ask   **33 rub** obstacle. (A term from bowls.)

Dear nurse of arts, plenties, and joyful births,
Should not in this best garden of the world,
Our fertile France, put up her lovely visage?   37
Alas, she hath from France too long been chased,
And all her husbandry doth lie on heaps,   39
Corrupting in its own fertility.
Her vine, the merry cheerer of the heart,
Unprunèd dies; her hedges even-pleached,   42
Like prisoners wildly overgrown with hair,
Put forth disordered twigs; her fallow leas   44
The darnel, hemlock, and rank fumitory   45
Doth root upon, while that the coulter rusts   46
That should deracinate such savagery.   47
The even mead, that erst brought sweetly forth   48
The freckled cowslip, burnet, and green clover,   49
Wanting the scythe, all uncorrected, rank,   50
Conceives by idleness, and nothing teems   51
But hateful docks, rough thistles, kecksies, burrs,   52
Losing both beauty and utility.
And all our vineyards, fallows, meads, and hedges,   54
Defective in their natures, grow to wildness.   55
Even so our houses and ourselves and children   56
Have lost, or do not learn for want of time,
The sciences that should become our country,   58
But grow like savages—as soldiers will
That nothing do but meditate on blood—
To swearing and stern looks, diffused attire,   61
And everything that seems unnatural.
Which to reduce into our former favor   63
You are assembled, and my speech entreats
That I may know the let why gentle Peace   65

---

37 put up show **39 husbandry** cultivated fields, agricultural produce
42 even-pleached smoothly intertwined **44 fallow leas** uncultivated
open fields **45 darnel . . . fumitory** i.e., weeds that grow in cultivated
land **46 coulter** cutting blade in front of the plowshare **47 deracinate**
root out **48 even mead** level meadow. **erst** formerly **49 burnet** a
herb **50 Wanting** lacking **51 Conceives** gives birth (to weeds). **teems**
flourishes **52 kecksies** dry-stemmed plants, possibly dried hemlock
stalks **54 fallows** land plowed and left lying **55 Defective . . . natures**
i.e., perverted from their natural function, which is to grow useful
plants **56 houses** households **58 sciences** skills **61 diffused** disordered **63 reduce . . . favor** return to our former good appearance
65 let hindrance

Should not expel these inconveniences
And bless us with her former qualities.

KING HENRY
  If, Duke of Burgundy, you would the peace,   68
  Whose want gives growth to th' imperfections   69
  Which you have cited, you must buy that peace
  With full accord to all our just demands,
  Whose tenors and particular effects   72
  You have enscheduled briefly in your hands.   73

BURGUNDY
  The King hath heard them, to the which as yet
  There is no answer made.

KING HENRY   Well then, the peace,
  Which you before so urged, lies in his answer.

FRENCH KING
  I have but with a cursitory eye   77
  O'erglanced the articles. Pleaseth Your Grace   78
  To appoint some of your council presently
  To sit with us once more, with better heed
  To re-survey them, we will suddenly   81
  Pass our accept and peremptory answer.   82

KING HENRY
  Brother, we shall. Go, uncle Exeter,
  And brother Clarence, and you, brother Gloucester,
  Warwick, and Huntingdon, go with the King,
  And take with you free power to ratify,
  Augment, or alter, as your wisdoms best
  Shall see advantageable for our dignity,   88
  Anything in or out of our demands,
  And we'll consign thereto.—Will you, fair sister,   90
  Go with the princes, or stay here with us?

QUEEN ISABEL
  Our gracious brother, I will go with them.
  Haply a woman's voice may do some good   93
  When articles too nicely urged be stood on.   94

68 would wish **69 want** lack **72 tenors** general purport. **particular
effects** specific details **73 enscheduled** drawn up in writing
77 cursitory cursory, hasty **78 Pleaseth** may it please **81 suddenly**
speedily **82 Pass . . . answer** deliver an answer acceptable to us and
final, decisive **88 advantageable** advantageous **90 consign** agree,
subscribe **93 Haply** perhaps **94 nicely** punctiliously, with insistence
on detail. **stood on** insisted on

KING HENRY
  Yet leave our cousin Katharine here with us.
  She is our capital demand, comprised   96
  Within the fore-rank of our articles.   97

QUEEN ISABEL
  She hath good leave.
               Exeunt omnes. Manent King [Henry]
                      and Katharine [with Alice].

KING HENRY   Fair Katharine, and most fair,   98
  Will you vouchsafe to teach a soldier terms
  Such as will enter at a lady's ear
  And plead his love suit to her gentle heart?

KATHARINE Your Majesty shall mock at me. I cannot
speak your England.

KING HENRY O fair Katharine, if you will love me
soundly with your French heart, I will be glad to hear
you confess it brokenly with your English tongue. Do
you like me, Kate?

KATHARINE *Pardonnez-moi,* I cannot tell wat is "like
me."

KING HENRY An angel is like you, Kate, and you are like
an angel.

KATHARINE [*To Alice*] *Que dit-il? Que je suis semblable*   112
à les anges?   113

ALICE *Oui, vraiment, sauf Votre Grâce, ainsi dit-il.*   114

KING HENRY I said so, dear Katharine; and I must not
blush to affirm it.

KATHARINE *O bon Dieu! Les langues des hommes sont
pleines de tromperies.*

KING HENRY What says she, fair one? That the tongues
of men are full of deceits?

ALICE *Oui,* dat de tongues of de mans is be full of deceits. Dat is de Princess.

KING HENRY The Princess is the better Englishwoman.   123
I' faith, Kate, my wooing is fit for thy understanding.
I am glad thou canst speak no better English, for if
thou couldst, thou wouldst find me such a plain king

---

96 capital chief **97 fore-rank** first row **98 s.d. omnes** all. **Manent**
they remain onstage **112–114 Que . . . ainsi dit-il** What does he say?
That I am like the angels? ALICE Yes, truly, save Your Grace, he says
so **123 the better Englishwoman** i.e., she has a true Englishwoman's
modesty and mistrust of flattery

that thou wouldst think I had sold my farm to buy my
crown. I know no ways to mince it in love, but directly 128
to say, "I love you." Then if you urge me farther than
to say, "Do you in faith?" I wear out my suit. Give me 130
your answer, i' faith, do, and so clap hands and a bar- 131
gain. How say you, lady?

KATHARINE   *Sauf votre honneur,* me understand well.

KING HENRY   Marry, if you would put me to verses or to
dance for your sake, Kate, why, you undid me. For the
one I have neither words nor measure, and for the 136
other I have no strength in measure, yet a reasonable 137
measure in strength. If I could win a lady at leapfrog, 138
or by vaulting into my saddle with my armor on my
back, under the correction of bragging be it spoken, I
should quickly leap into a wife. Or if I might buffet for 141
my love, or bound my horse for her favors, I could lay 142
on like a butcher and sit like a jackanapes, never off. 143
But before God, Kate, I cannot look greenly, nor gasp 144
out my eloquence, nor I have no cunning in protesta-
tion—only downright oaths, which I never use till 146
urged, nor never break for urging. If thou canst love a
fellow of this temper, Kate, whose face is not worth 148
sunburning, that never looks in his glass for love of 149
anything he sees there, let thine eye be thy cook. I 150
speak to thee plain soldier. If thou canst love me for
this, take me. If not, to say to thee that I shall die is
true; but for thy love, by the Lord, no. Yet I love thee
too. And while thou liv'st, dear Kate, take a fellow of
plain and uncoined constancy, for he perforce must do 155
thee right, because he hath not the gift to woo in other
places. For these fellows of infinite tongue that can
rhyme themselves into ladies' favors, they do always
reason themselves out again. What? A speaker is but
a prater, a rhyme is but a ballad. A good leg will fall, 160

128 mince it speak coyly **130 wear out my suit** expend all my resources as a wooer **131 clap** clasp **136 measure** meter **137 measure**
dance **138 measure** amount **141 buffet** box **142 bound** make
prance **143 jackanapes** ape, monkey **144 greenly** like a lovesick
youth **146 downright** straightforward **148–149 not worth sunburning**
i.e., so ugly that the sun couldn't make it worse **150 cook** (She must
dress him with fine qualities as a cook dresses meat.) **155 uncoined**
not coined for circulation; also, unalloyed, therefore fixed, steady
160 fall shrink, lose its shapeliness

a straight back will stoop, a black beard will turn
white, a curled pate will grow bald, a fair face will
wither, a full eye will wax hollow; but a good heart,
Kate, is the sun and the moon—or rather the sun and
not the moon, for it shines bright and never changes,
but keeps his course truly. If thou would have such a
one, take me. And take me, take a soldier; take a soldier, take a king. And what sayst thou then to my
love? Speak, my fair, and fairly, I pray thee.

KATHARINE Is it possible dat I sould love de *ennemi* of
France?

KING HENRY No, it is not possible you should love the
enemy of France, Kate; but in loving me you should
love the friend of France, for I love France so well that
I will not part with a village of it. I will have it all mine.
And, Kate, when France is mine and I am yours, then
yours is France and you are mine.

KATHARINE I cannot tell wat is dat.

KING HENRY No, Kate? I will tell thee in French, which
I am sure will hang upon my tongue like a new-mar-
ried wife about her husband's neck, hardly to be
shook off. *Je quand sur le possession de France, et*   182
quand vous avez le possession de moi—let me see,
what then? Saint Denis be my speed!—*donc vôtre est*   184
France et vous êtes mienne. It is as easy for me, Kate,   185
to conquer the kingdom as to speak so much more
French. I shall never move thee in French, unless it be
to laugh at me.

KATHARINE *Sauf votre honneur, le français que vous*   189
parlez, il est meilleur que l'anglais lequel je parle.   190

KING HENRY No, faith, is 't not, Kate. But thy speaking
of my tongue, and I thine, most truly-falsely, must   192
needs be granted to be much at one. But, Kate, dost   193
thou understand thus much English: Canst thou
love me?

KATHARINE I cannot tell.

KING HENRY Can any of your neighbors tell, Kate? I'll

182–185 Je . . . mienne (Henry haltingly translates the last sentence in
his previous speech.) **184 Saint Denis** patron saint of France. **be my
speed** help me **189–190 Sauf . . . parle** save your honor, the French that
you speak is better than the English that I speak **192 truly-falsely**
truthfully but incorrectly **193 at one** alike

ask them. Come, I know thou lovest me. And at night,
when you come into your closet, you'll question this   199
gentlewoman about me; and I know, Kate, you will to
her dispraise those parts in me that you love with your
heart. But, good Kate, mock me mercifully, the rather,
gentle Princess, because I love thee cruelly. If ever thou
beest mine, Kate, as I have a saving faith within me
tells me thou shalt, I get thee with scambling, and thou   205
must therefore needs prove a good soldier-breeder.
Shall not thou and I, between Saint Denis and Saint
George, compound a boy, half French, half English,
that shall go to Constantinople and take the Turk by
the beard? Shall we not? What sayst thou, my fair
flower-de-luce?   211

KATHARINE   I do not know dat.

KING HENRY   No; 'tis hereafter to know, but now to
promise. Do but now promise, Kate, you will endeavor for your French part of such a boy, and for my
English moiety take the word of a king and a bachelor.
How answer you, *la plus belle Katharine du monde,*   217
mon très cher et devin déesse?   218

KATHARINE   Your Majestee 'ave *fausse* French enough to   219
deceive de most *sage demoiselle* dat is *en France.*

KING HENRY   Now, fie upon my false French! By mine
honor, in true English, I love thee, Kate; by which
honor I dare not swear thou lovest me, yet my blood
begins to flatter me that thou dost, notwithstanding
the poor and untempering effect of my visage. Now   225
beshrew my father's ambition! He was thinking of
civil wars when he got me; therefore was I created
with a stubborn outside, with an aspect of iron, that   228
when I come to woo ladies I fright them. But in faith,
Kate, the elder I wax the better I shall appear. My
comfort is that old age, that ill layer-up of beauty, can
do no more spoil upon my face. Thou hast me, if thou
hast me, at the worst; and thou shalt wear me, if thou
wear me, better and better. And therefore tell me,

---

199 **closet** private chamber   205 **scambling** scrambling, struggling
211 **flower-de-luce** fleur-de-lis, the emblem of France   217–218 **la plus
. . . déesse** the most beautiful Katharine in the world, my very dear and
divine goddess   219 **fausse** i.e., false (both "incorrect" and "decep-
tive")   225 **untempering** unsoftening   228 **aspect** appearance

most fair Katharine, will you have me? Put off your
maiden blushes; avouch the thoughts of your heart 236
with the looks of an empress; take me by the hand,
and say, "Harry of England, I am thine." Which word
thou shalt no sooner bless mine ear withal, but I will
tell thee aloud, "England is thine, Ireland is thine,
France is thine, and Henry Plantagenet is thine"—
who, though I speak it before his face, if he be not
fellow with the best king, thou shalt find the best king
of good fellows. Come, your answer in broken music! 244
For thy voice is music, and thy English broken. Therefore, queen of all, Katharine, break thy mind to me in 246
broken English. Wilt thou have me?

KATHARINE   Dat is as it shall please de *roi mon père.*   248

KING HENRY   Nay, it will please him well, Kate. It shall
please him, Kate.

KATHARINE   Den it sall also content me.

KING HENRY   Upon that I kiss your hand, and I call you
my queen.   [*He attempts to kiss her hand.*]

KATHARINE   *Laissez, mon seigneur, laissez, laissez! Ma* 254
foi, je ne veux point que vous abaissiez votre grandeur 255
en baisant la main d'une—Notre Seigneur!—indigne 256
serviteur. Excusez-moi, je vous supplie, mon très 257
puissant seigneur. 258

KING HENRY   Then I will kiss your lips, Kate.

KATHARINE   *Les dames et demoiselles pour être baisées* 260
devant leur noces, il n'est pas la coutume de France. 261

KING HENRY   [*To Alice*] Madam my interpreter, what
says she?

ALICE   Dat it is not be de fashion *pour les* ladies of
France—I cannot tell wat is *baiser en* Anglish.

KING HENRY   To kiss.

ALICE   Your Majestee *entendre* bettre *que moi.*   267

KING HENRY   It is not a fashion for the maids in France
to kiss before they are married, would she say?

---

236 avouch guarantee   **244 broken music** music in parts   **246 break**
open   **248 de roi mon père** the King my father   **254–258 Laissez . . .**
seigneur don't, my lord, don't, don't; by my faith, I do not wish to lower
your greatness by kissing the hand of an—Our dear Lord!—unworthy
servant; excuse me, I beg you, my most powerful lord   **260–261 Les**
dames . . . France it is not customary in France for ladies and young
girls to be kissed before their marriage   **267 entendre . . . moi** under-
stands better than I

ALICE   *Oui, vraiment.*   270
KING HENRY   O Kate, nice customs curtsy to great kings. 271
Dear Kate, you and I cannot be confined within the
weak list of a country's fashion. We are the makers of 273
manners, Kate; and the liberty that follows our places 274
stops the mouth of all find-faults, as I will do yours,
for upholding the nice fashion of your country in de-
nying me a kiss. Therefore, patiently and yielding.
[*He kisses her.*] You have witchcraft in your lips, Kate.
There is more eloquence in a sugar touch of them than
in the tongues of the French council, and they should
sooner persuade Harry of England than a general pe-
tition of monarchs.—Here comes your father.

Enter the French power and the English lords.

BURGUNDY   God save Your Majesty! My royal cousin,
teach you our princess English?
KING HENRY   I would have her learn, my fair cousin,
how perfectly I love her, and that is good English.
BURGUNDY   Is she apt?
KING HENRY   Our tongue is rough, coz, and my condi- 288
tion is not smooth; so that, having neither the voice 289
nor the heart of flattery about me, I cannot so conjure
up the spirit of love in her that he will appear in his
true likeness.
BURGUNDY   Pardon the frankness of my mirth, if I answer you for that. If you would conjure in her, you 294
must make a circle; if conjure up love in her in his true
likeness, he must appear naked and blind. Can you
blame her then, being a maid yet rosed over with the 297
virgin crimson of modesty, if she deny the appearance
of a naked blind boy in her naked seeing self? It were,
my lord, a hard condition for a maid to consign to. 300
KING HENRY   Yet they do wink and yield, as love is 301
blind and enforces.
BURGUNDY   They are then excused, my lord, when they
see not what they do.

270 Oui, vraiment yes, truly   **271 nice** fastidious   **273 list** limit, bar-
rier   **274 follows our places** attends our (high) rank   **288–289 condition**
personality   **294 conjure in her** (with bawdy double meaning, continued
in *circle, hard,* etc.)   **297 yet rosed over** still blushing   **300 consign**
agree   **301 wink** close the eyes

KING HENRY   Then, good my lord, teach your cousin to consent winking.

BURGUNDY   I will wink on her to consent, my lord, if you will teach her to know my meaning; for maids, well summered and warm kept, are like flies at Bar- 309 tholomew-tide: blind, though they have their eyes, and 310 then they will endure handling, which before would not abide looking on.

KING HENRY   This moral ties me over to time and a hot summer; and so I shall catch the fly, your cousin, in the latter end, and she must be blind too.

BURGUNDY   As love is, my lord, before it loves.   316

KING HENRY   It is so; and you may, some of you, thank love for my blindness, who cannot see many a fair 318 French city for one fair French maid that stands in 319 my way.   320

FRENCH KING   Yes, my lord, you see them perspectively, 321 the cities turned into a maid; for they are all girdled with maiden walls that war hath never entered.   323

KING HENRY   Shall Kate be my wife?

FRENCH KING   So please you.

KING HENRY   I am content, so the maiden cities you talk of may wait on her. So the maid that stood in the way 327 for my wish shall show me the way to my will.

FRENCH KING
  We have consented to all terms of reason.

KING HENRY   Is 't so, my lords of England?

WESTMORLAND
  The King hath granted every article:
  His daughter first, and then in sequel all,
  According to their firm proposèd natures.   333

EXETER
  Only he hath not yet subscribèd this: 334

309 summered nurtured   **309–310 Bartholomew-tide** August 24 (when flies, bees, etc., are sluggish)   **316 As . . . loves** (Love is blind before it loves because it cannot yet see the beloved, and because love has not yet opened the lover's eyes.)   **318–320 who . . . my way** (i.e., Henry is willing to forgo several French cities in exchange for Katharine that he might otherwise take possession of in the negotiations.)
321 perspectively i.e., distorted by a perspective glass   **323 maiden** unbreached   **327 wait on her** attend her, go along with her (as part of her dowry)   **333 According . . . natures** exactly as specified in the proposals   **334 subscribèd** agreed to

Where Your Majesty demands that the King of France,
having any occasion to write for matter of grant, shall 336
name Your Highness in this form and with this addi- 337
tion, in French, *Notre très cher fils Henri, Roi* 338
d'Angleterre, Héritier de France; and thus in Latin, 339
Praeclarissimus filius noster Henricus, Rex Angliae
et Haeres Franciae.

FRENCH KING
Nor this I have not, brother, so denied   342
But your request shall make me let it pass.   343

KING HENRY
I pray you then, in love and dear alliance,
Let that one article rank with the rest,
And thereupon give me your daughter.

FRENCH KING
Take her, fair son, and from her blood raise up
Issue to me, that the contending kingdoms
Of France and England, whose very shores look pale
With envy of each other's happiness,
May cease their hatred, and this dear conjunction
Plant neighborhood and Christian-like accord
In their sweet bosoms, that never war advance
His bleeding sword twixt England and fair France.

LORDS Amen!

KING HENRY
Now, welcome, Kate; and bear me witness all,
That here I kiss her as my sovereign queen. [*Kiss.*]
                                        Flourish.

QUEEN ISABEL
God, the best maker of all marriages,
Combine your hearts in one, your realms in one!
As man and wife, being two, are one in love,
So be there twixt your kingdoms such a spousal   361
That never may ill office, or fell jealousy,   362
Which troubles oft the bed of blessèd marriage,
Thrust in between the paction of these kingdoms   364
To make divorce of their incorporate league;

336 **for . . . grant** in official deeds granting title to land and the like
337–338 **addition** title   338–339 **Notre . . . France** our very dear son
Henry, King of England, Heir of France   342 **so** so firmly   343 **But** but
that   361 **spousal** marriage   362 **ill office** unfriendly dealings. **fell**
cruel   364 **paction** alliance, compact

That English may as French, French Englishmen,
Receive each other. God speak this "Amen"!

ALL   Amen!

KING HENRY
Prepare we for our marriage, on which day,
My lord of Burgundy, we'll take your oath,
And all the peers', for surety of our leagues.
Then shall I swear to Kate, and you to me;
And may our oaths well kept and prosperous be!

Sennet.   Exeunt.

❖

Epilogue   *Enter Chorus.*

CHORUS
Thus far, with rough and all-unable pen,
   Our bending author hath pursued the story,   2
In little room confining mighty men,
   Mangling by starts the full course of their glory.   4
Small time, but in that small most greatly lived   5
   This star of England. Fortune made his sword,
By which the world's best garden he achieved,   7
   And of it left his son imperial lord.
Henry the Sixth, in infant bands crowned King   9
   Of France and England, did this king succeed;
Whose state so many had the managing
   That they lost France and made his England bleed,
Which oft our stage hath shown; and, for their sake,   13
In your fair minds let this acceptance take.   [*Exit*.]   14

Epilogue.
2 bending i.e., under the weight of his task   **4 by starts** in fits and
starts, in fragments   **5 Small time** (Henry V ruled for only nine years,
dying at the age of thirty-five.)   **7 best garden** i.e., France   **9 infant
bands** swaddling clothes   **13 Which . . . shown** (Refers to the three parts
of *King Henry VI*.)   **for their sake** i.e., since you liked them   **14 this
acceptance take** this play meet with your approval

Date and Text

An entry in the Stationers' Register, the official record book of the London Company of Stationers (booksellers and printers), for August 4, 1600, provides that "Henry the ffift" and three other plays belonging to the Lord Chamberlain's men (Shakespeare's acting company) are "to be staied" from publication until further permission is granted. Evidently the Chamberlain's men were anxious to prevent unauthorized publication. They did not succeed, however, in preventing the appearance of a pirated text of *Henry V*. An entry in the Stationers' Register for August 14 assigns to Thomas Pavier an already published work entitled "The historye of Henry the Vth with the battell of Agencourt." The quarto volume to which this entry refers is the following:

> THE CHRONICLE History of Henry the fift, With his battell fought at *Agin Court* in *France*. Togither with *Auntient Pistoll. As it hath bene sundry times playd by the Right honorable the Lord Chamberlaine his seruants*. LONDON Printed by *Thomas Creede*, for Tho. Millington, and Iohn Busby. And are to be sold at his house in Carter Lane, next the Powle head. 1600.

The text of this play is manifestly corrupt. It is considerably shorter than the First Folio version and completely omits the choruses and three entire scenes (1.1, 3.1, and 4.2). The remainder seems to have been put together by memorial reconstruction. This bad quarto served as the basis for a second quarto printed by Thomas Creede for Thomas Pavier in 1602 and a third printed by William Jaggard for Thomas Pavier in 1619 but fraudulently dated 1608. The Folio text was printed seemingly from an authorial manuscript, perhaps with occasional reference to the third quarto (which contains some potentially troublesome contamination). The Folio text is thus the most reliable version, though the first quarto is also an interesting witness, especially for visual effects recorded in its stage directions, for a few readings in the text, and for verse lineation of Pistol's speeches.

Francis Meres does not mention the play in 1598 in his

Palladis Tamia: Wit's Treasury (a slender volume on contemporary literature and art; valuable because it lists most of the plays of Shakespeare's that existed at that time), though he does mention *"Henry the IV."* The epilogue to *2 Henry IV* (written probably in·1597) promises that "our humble author will continue the story, with Sir John in it, and make you merry with fair Katharine of France"; and since the prediction is not really accurate regarding Falstaff, we can be reasonably certain that Shakespeare had not yet begun *Henry V* in 1597. An allusion in the chorus of Act 5 to "the General of our gracious Empress," who may in good time come home from Ireland with "rebellion broachèd on his sword," has been taken by virtually all editors to refer to the Earl of Essex, who left in March of 1599 to quell the Irish rebellion headed by Tyrone. Although Essex returned on September 28 of that same year having failed utterly in his assignment, the departure of such a charismatic figure could have inspired Shakespeare's praising remark. A minority view holds that the choruses (which do not appear in the bad quarto of 1600) could have been written later in 1601 for Essex's far more victorious successor, Lord Mountjoy (see Warren D. Smith's article on *Henry V* in *JEGP*, 1954). Still, Essex was more center stage during those exciting years, more likely to have been the subject of adulation. In any case the play itself must have been written before August of 1600, most probably in 1599. The reference to "this wooden O" in the Chorus of Act 1 is often thought to be Shakespeare's compliment to the company's new theater, the Globe, which was ready for their use probably in 1599; but the play may have been produced at the Curtain instead.

Textual Notes

These textual notes are not a historical collation, either of the early quartos and folios or of more recent editions; they are simply a record of departures in this edition from the copy text. The reading adopted in this edition appears in boldface, followed by the rejected reading from the copy text, i.e., the First Folio. Only major alterations in punctuation are noted. Changes in lineation are not indicated, nor are some minor and obvious typographical errors.

Abbreviations used:
F the First Folio
Q the quarto of 1600
s.d. stage direction
s.p. speech prefix

Copy text: the First Folio.

Prologue.1 s.p. Chorus [not in F; also in prologues to other acts]

1.2. 38 succedant succedaul   **45 Elbe** Elue [also at l. 52]   **115 s.p. Ely** Bish
131 blood Bloods   **163 her** their   **166 s.p. A Lord** Bish. Ely   **197 majesty**
Maiesties   **212 End** [Q] And   **237 s.p. First Ambassador** Amb [also at l. 245]
310 s.d. Flourish [at the beginning of 2.0 in F]

2.1. 23 mare [Q] name   **28 s.p. Nym** [Q; not in F]   **42, 43 Iceland** Island
73 thee defy [Q] defie thee   **80 enough** enough to   **83 you** your
105–106 [Q; not in F]   **betting** beating [Q]   **116 that's** that

2.2. 29 s.p. Grey Kni   **87 furnish him** furnish   **107 a** an   **108 whoop** hoope
114 All And   **139 mark the** make thee   **147 Henry** [Q] Thomas   **148 Masham**
[Q] Marsham   **159 Which I** Which   **176 have sought** [Q] sought
181 s.d. Exeunt Exit

2.3. 16 'a babbled a Table   **24 upward** vp-peer'd   **32 s.p. Hostess** Woman
48 word world

2.4. 1 s.p. [and elsewhere] French King King   **132 Louvre** Louer
146 s.d. Flourish [at the beginning of 3.0 in F]

3.0. [here F has "Actus Secundus"]   **6 fanning** fayning   **35 eke** eech

3.1. 7 conjure commune   **17 noblest** Noblish   **24 men** me   **32 Straining**
Straying

3.2. 25 runs wins   **67 s.p. [and elsewhere in scene] Fluellen** Welch
82 s.p. [and elsewhere in scene] Jamy Scot   **87 s.p. [and elsewhere
in scene] Macmorris** Irish   **102 quite** quit   **112 Chrish** Christ

3.3. 32 heady headly   **35 Defile** Desire   **43** [here F has s.d. "Enter Gouer-
nour"]   **54 all. For** all for

3.4. 1–2 parles bien bien parlas [throughout the play, the French has been
somewhat modernized, besides the emendations listed here]   **8 Et les doigts**
[assigned to Alice in F]   **9 s.p. Alice** Kat   **les doigts** e doyt   **10 souviendrai**

souemeray **12 s.p. Katharine** Alice **13 j'ai** Kath. l'ay **16 Nous** [not in F]
40 pas déjà y desia **42 Non** Nome **46 Sauf** Sans

3.5. 11 de du **26 "Poor"** may Poore **43 Vaudemont** Vandemont **45 Foix**
Loys **46 knights** Kings

3.6. 31 her [Q] his **37 is make** [Q] makes **111–112 lenity** Leuitie

3.7. 12 pasterns postures **14 qui a** ches **59 lief** liue **65 et** est **truie** leuye

4.0. [here F has "Actus Tertius"] **16 name** nam'd **20 cripple** creeple
27 Presenteth Presented

4.1. 3 Good God **95 Thomas** Iohn **158 deaths** [Q] death **propose** purpose
227 s.d. Exeunt Exit [at l. 222 in F] **243 adoration** Odoration **289 ere** of
307 friends friend

4.2. 4 eaux ewes **6 Cieux** cein **47 drooping** dropping **49 gimmaled** Iymold

4.3. 12 [placed after l. 14 in F] **48** [Q; not in F] **124 'em** vm

4.4. 2 êtes estes le **15 Or** for **36 à cette heure** asture **37 couper** couppes
54 l'avez layt a **57 remercîments** remercious **58 j'ai tombé** Ie intombe
59 très-distingué tres distinie **68 Suivez-vous** Saaue-vous

4.5. 2 perdu . . . perdu perdia . . . perdie **3 Mort de** Mor Dieu **16 by a** [Q] a
base **24 s.d. Exeunt** Exit

4.6. 34 mistful mixtfull

4.7. [F has "Actus Quartus" here] **69 s.p.** [and elsewhere in this scene]
Montjoy Her **77 the** with **109 countryman** Countrymen **114 God** Good
123 'a live aliue [also in l. 126] **161 an 't** and

4.8. 100 Vaudemont Vandemont **113 we** me **121 in my** [Q] my

5.0. 29 but but by

5.1. 39 By Jesu [Q] I say **69 begun** began **88 swear** swore

5.2. 1 s.p. [and throughout scene] **King Henry** King **12 s.p.** [and throughout
scene] **Queen Isabel** Quee **12 England** Ireland **21 s.p.** [also elsewhere]
King Henry Eng **50 all** withall **61 diffused** defused **77 cursitory** curse-
larie **98 s.d. Manent** Manet **114 s.p.** [and elsewhere] **Alice** Lady **190 meilleur** melieus **265 baiser** buisse **323 hath never** hath **364 paction** Pation

Epilogue s.p. Chorus [not in F]

Shakespeare's Sources

Shakespeare's principal historical source for *Henry V*, as for *Richard II* and the *Henry IV* plays, was the 1587 edition of Raphael Holinshed's *Chronicles*. Holinshed's account of Henry V, however, had depended so heavily on Edward Hall's *The Union of the two Noble and Illustre Families of Lancaster and York* (1542) that we sometimes have difficulty knowing whether Shakespeare consulted Holinshed or Hall. He was certainly familiar with both. Shakespeare's sources all acclaim Henry V a hero-king. Samuel Daniel's *The First Four Books of the Civil Wars* (1595), which Shakespeare may have used for his account of the treasonous plot against Henry (2.2), also praises the King in encomiastic terms.

Shakespeare follows the order of events laid down in Holinshed and Hall: the personal rivalry between Henry and the French Dauphin, Henry's request for reassurance from the clergy as to the legitimacy of the war, the maneuvering of the clergy to forestall a bill in Parliament threatening to seize church land, the foiling of a plot against Henry's life, the siege of Harfleur, the glorious victory at Agincourt. Both Holinshed and Hall offer Shakespeare many particulars about the English claim to France: in both accounts, the Archbishop quotes the law—*In terram Salicam mulieres ne succedant*—and goes on at length about King Pharamond, the rivers Elbe and Saale, King Pepin, Hugh Capet, the Book of Numbers, and the rest. On the other hand, Shakespeare omits a three-year campaign that historically intervened between Agincourt and the peace treaty of Troyes. He passes over the Lollard controversy in England, with the execution of Sir John Oldcastle. And, of course, he adds unforgettable characters that we do not find in the chronicles—Welshmen, Irishmen, Scots, common soldiers, thieves—who show the unity of the British nation under King Henry's charismatic leadership.

For many of his additions to the chronicles, Shakespeare was indebted to the anonymous *The Famous Victories of Henry the Fifth* (c. 1588). This old play, not registered until 1594 and not printed until 1598, exists today only in a corrupt text; quite possibly Shakespeare knew a fuller and more authentic version that would have given him still more material. Other plays may have existed on the subject, for the Admiral's men (a rival acting company) acted a "harey the v" in 1595 and 1596 that may or may not have been *The Famous Victories.* In any event, the relationship between *Henry V* and *Famous Victories* is at times close. *Famous Victories* omits Henry's long campaign between Agincourt and the final peace treaty, as does Shakespeare's play. The Archbishop of *Famous Victories* discusses the French claim just before the arrival of the French Ambassador with the tennis balls. (In Holinshed, the tennis-ball incident occurs first, at Kenilworth, whereas the Archbishop's lecture occurs sometime later at a meeting of Parliament in Leicester.) Henry assures the French Ambassador that he has "free liberty and license to speak." To the Dauphin's insolent gift, taunting Henry about his wild youth, the King suavely replies that "My lord prince Dauphin is very pleasant with me," and promises to repay the insult with balls of brass and iron. (Holinshed mentions this apparently nonhistorical legend only briefly.) When the French noblemen assembled at the French court hear of Henry's arrival on their shores, they tremble with fear even though the Dauphin recklessly scoffs at so young and prodigal a king. Henry is accompanied to France by a ludicrous assortment of London artisans and thieves, such as John Cobbler, who bids farewell to his wife in a comic scene similar to Pistol's parting from the Hostess, and Derick, who turns the tables on a French soldier much as Pistol deals with Monsieur le Fer. When King Henry woos Katharine of France, he protests to her that he cannot speak flatteringly because he is a plain soldier. She asks in return: "How should I love him that hath dealt so hardly / With my father?" Despite these resemblances, however, Shakespeare's *Henry V* is incomparably superior to the old play and contains many original scenes and characters, such as King Henry's touring of his camp incognito, the quarrel between Henry and Williams, and above all the scenes involving Fluellen and his fellow-captains.

Other possible sources include the *Henrici Quinti Angliae Regis Gesta* written by a chaplain in Henry V's army, the *Vita et Gesta Henrici Quinti* erroneously ascribed to Thomas Elmham, the *Vita Henrici Quinti* by "Titus Livius," translated 1513 (in which the French brag about their horses and armor), a ballad called "The Battle of Agincourt" (c. 1530), and *The Annals of Cornelius Tacitus*, translated 1598 (in which Germanicus walks disguised through his camp at night "to sound the soldiers' mind" and hears his leadership praised).

The Third Volume of Chronicles (1587 edition)
Compiled by Raphael Holinshed

HENRY THE FIFTH

[Holinshed begins with an account of Henry's birth, his reformation, his coronation, and his banishment of the "misruly mates of dissolute order and life" he had known before. The King orders that King Richard II's body and that of Anne, his first wife, be reinterred at Westminster with great ceremony.]

Whilst in the Lent season[1] the King lay[2] at Kenilworth,* there came to him from Charles, Dauphin of France, certain ambassadors, that brought with them a barrel of Paris balls,[3] which from their master they presented to him for a token that was taken in very ill part, as sent in scorn to signify that it was more meet for the King to pass the time with such childish exercise than to attempt any worthy exploit. Wherefore the King wrote to him that ere aught long he would toss him some London balls that perchance should shake the walls of the best court in France. . . .

In the second year of his reign, King Henry called his high court of Parliament, the last day of April,[4] in the town of Leicester, in which Parliament many profitable laws were concluded, and many petitions moved were for that time deferred. Amongst which one was that a bill exhibited in the Parliament holden at Westminster in the eleventh year of King Henry the Fourth (which, by reason the King was then troubled with civil discord, came to none effect) might now with good deliberation be pondered and brought to some good conclusion. The effect of which supplication was that the temporal lands devoutly given and disordinately[5] spent by religious and other spiritual persons should be seized into the King's hands, sith[6] the same might suffice to maintain, to the honor of the King and defense of the realm, fifteen earls, fifteen hundred knights, six thou-

---

1 **Lent season** (in early 1414) 2 **lay** resided 3 **Paris balls** tennis balls
4 **April** (in 1414) 5 **disordinately** prodigally, inordinately 6 **sith** since

sand and two hundred esquires, and a hundred almshouses for relief only of the poor, impotent, and needy persons, and the King to have clearly[7] to his coffers twenty thousand pounds, with many other provisions and values of religious houses which I pass over.

This bill was much noted and more feared among the religious sort, whom surely it touched very near, and therefore, to find remedy against it, they determined to assay all ways to put by and overthrow this bill; wherein they thought best to try if they might move the King's mood with some sharp invention, that he should not regard the importunate petitions of the commons. Whereupon, on a day in the Parliament, Henry Chichele, Archbishop of Canterbury, made a pithy oration wherein he declared how not only the duchies of Normandy and Aquitaine with the counties of Anjou and Maine and the country of Gascony were by undoubted title appertaining to the King, as to the lawful and only heir of the same, but also the whole realm of France, as heir to his great-grandfather, King Edward the Third.

Herein did he much inveigh against the surmised[8] and false feigned law Salic, which the Frenchmen allege ever against the kings of England in bar of their just title to the crown of France. The very words of that supposed law are these: *In terram Salicam mulieres ne succedant*, that is to say, "Into the Salic land let not women succeed." Which the French glossers expound to be the realm of France, and that this law was made by King Pharamond; whereas yet their own authors affirm that the land Salic is in Germany, between the rivers of Elbe and Saale, and that when Charles the Great had overcome the Saxons he placed there certain Frenchmen, which having in disdain the dishonest[9] manners of the German women, made a law that the females should not succeed to any inheritance within that land, which at this day is called Meissen. So that, if this be true, this law was not made for the realm of France, nor the Frenchmen possessed the land Salic till four hundred and one-and-twenty years after the death of Pharamond, the supposed maker of this Salic law; for this Pharamond deceased in the year 426, and Charles the Great subdued the

---

7 clearly entirely   **8 surmised** devised falsely   **9 dishonest** unchaste

Saxons and placed the Frenchmen in those parts beyond the river of Saale in the year 805.

Moreover, it appeareth by their own writers that King Pepin, which deposed Childeric, claimed the crown of France as heir general for that he was descended of Blithild, daughter to King Clothair the First. Hugh Capet also, who usurped the crown upon[10] Charles, Duke of Lorraine, the sole heir male of the line and stock of Charles the Great, to make his title seem true and appear good, though indeed it was stark naught, conveyed himself as heir to the Lady Lingard, daughter to King Charlemagne, son to Lewis the Emperor that was son to Charles the Great. King Lewis also, the Tenth,[11] otherwise called Saint Lewis, being very heir to the said usurper Hugh Capet, could never be satisfied in his conscience how he might justly keep and possess the crown of France till he was persuaded and fully instructed that Queen Isabel his grandmother was lineally descended of the Lady Ermengard, daughter and heir to the above-named Charles, Duke of Lorraine, by the which marriage the blood and line of Charles the Great was again united and restored to the crown and scepter of France; so that more clear than the sun it openly appeareth that the title of King Pepin, the claim of Hugh Capet, the possession of Lewis, yea, and the French kings to this day, are derived and conveyed from the heir female, though they would under the color of such a feigned law bar the kings and princes of this realm of England of their right and lawful inheritance.

The Archbishop further alleged out of the Book of Numbers this saying: "When a man dyeth without a son, let the inheritance descend to his daughter." At length, having said sufficiently for the proof of the King's just and lawful title to the crown of France, he exhorted him to advance forth his banner to fight for his right, to conquer his inheritance, to spare neither blood, sword, nor fire, sith his war was just, his cause good, and his claim true. And to the intent his loving chaplains and obedient subjects of the spirituality might show themselves willing and desirous to aid His Majesty for the recovery of his ancient right and true

10 **upon** from   11 **Tenth** (Actually Ninth; an error in Holinshed which Shakespeare copies in 1.2.77.)

inheritance, the Archbishop declared that in their spiritual convocation they had granted to His Highness such a sum of money as never by no spiritual persons was to any prince before those days given or advanced.

When the Archbishop had ended his prepared tale, Ralph Neville, Earl of Westmorland and as then Lord Warden of the Marches against Scotland, understanding that the King, upon a courageous desire to recover his right in France, would surely take the wars in hand, thought good to move the King to begin first with Scotland, and thereupon declared how easy a matter it should be to make a conquest there and how greatly the same should further his wished purpose for the subduing of the Frenchmen, concluding the sum of his tale with this old saying, that "Whoso will France win, must with Scotland first begin." Many matters he touched, as well to show how necessary the conquest of Scotland should be as also to prove how just a cause the King had to attempt it, trusting to persuade the King and all other to be of his opinion.

But after he had made an end, the Duke of Exeter, uncle to the King, a man well learned and wise (who had been sent into Italy by his father, intending that he should have been a priest), replied against the Earl of Westmorland's oration, affirming rather that he which would Scotland win, he with France must first begin. For if the King might once compass the conquest of France, Scotland could not long resist; so that conquer France, and Scotland would soon obey. For where should the Scots learn policy and skill to defend themselves if they had not their bringing up and training in France? If the French pensions maintained not the Scottish nobility, in what case should they be? Then take away France and the Scots will soon be tamed, France being to Scotland the same that the sap is to the tree, which being taken away the tree must needs die and wither.

To be brief, the Duke of Exeter used such earnest and pithy persuasions to induce the King and the whole assembly of the Parliament to credit his words that immediately after he had made an end all the company began to cry, "War! War! France! France!" Hereby the bill for dissolving of religious houses was clearly set aside and nothing thought on but only the recovering of France, according as the Archbishop had moved.

[At this Parliament, continued at Westminster, the King makes his uncle John the Duke of Bedford, his brother Humphrey the Duke of Gloucester, and Thomas Beaufort, Marquess Dorset, the Duke of Exeter. Meantime English ambassadors present Henry's demands to the French King, offering a marriage between King Henry and Lady Katharine of France in return for the surrender of certain French territories claimed by the English. The English ambassadors return to England with no answer as yet from the French, and Henry determines to prepare an invasion. The French, led by the Dauphin because his father "was fallen into his old disease of frenzy," prepare to resist. They send an embassage meanwhile to Henry with counterproposals (including still the marriage of Lady Katharine and Henry), but the offer of territories is insufficient and is refused. Henry replies to the French ambassador, the Archbishop of Bourges, in ringing terms:]

"I little esteem your French brags and less set[12] by your power and strength; I know perfectly my right to my region, which you usurp; and except[13] you deny the apparent[14] truth, so do yourselves also.[15] If you neither do nor will know it, yet God and the world knoweth it. The power of your master you see, but my puissance ye have not yet tasted. If he have loving subjects, I am, I thank God, not unstored of the same;[16] and I say this unto you, that before one year pass, I trust to make the highest crown of your country to stoop and the proudest miter to learn his humiliatedo.[17] In the meantime tell this to the usurper your master, that within three months I will enter into France as into mine own true and lawful patrimony, appointing[18] to acquire the same not with brag of words but with deeds of men and dint of sword by the aid of God, in whom is my whole trust and confidence. Further matter at this present I impart not unto you, saving that with warrant you may depart surely and safely into your country, where I trust sooner to visit you than you shall have cause to bid me wel-

---

12 less set set even less store   13 except unless   14 apparent self-evident   15 so . . . also i.e., you know it just as well as I do   16 not . . . same i.e., not lacking in loving subjects of my own   17 his humiliatedo its humiliation   18 appointing preparing

come." With this answer the ambassadors, sore displeased in their minds although they were highly entertained and liberally rewarded, departed into their country, reporting to the Dauphin how they had sped.[19]

[The King makes preparations to defend England against the Scots during the French campaign. Leaving the realm under the governance of his stepmother, the Queen Mother, Henry proceeds to Southampton and dispatches one last embassy to the French.]

When King Henry had fully furnished his navy with men, munition, and other provisions, perceiving that his captains misliked nothing so much as delay, he* determined his soldiers to go[20] a-shipboard and away. But see the hap! The night before the day appointed for their departure, he was credibly informed that Richard, Earl of Cambridge, brother to Edward, Duke of York, and Henry, Lord Scroop of Masham, Lord Treasurer, with Thomas Grey, a knight of Northumberland, being confederate together, had conspired his death. Wherefore he caused them to be apprehended. The said Lord Scroop was in such favor with the King that he admitted him sometimes to be his bedfellow, in whose fidelity the King reposed such trust that when any private or public counsel was in hand, this lord had much in the determination of it. For he represented so great gravity in his countenance, such modesty in behavior, and so virtuous zeal to all godliness in his talk that whatsoever he said was thought for the most part necessary to be done and followed. Also the said Sir Thomas Grey, as some write, was of the King's Privy Council.

These prisoners, upon their examination, confessed that for a great sum of money which they had received of the French King, they intended verily either to have delivered the King alive into the hands of his enemies or else to have murdered him before he should arrive in the duchy of Normandy. When King Henry had heard all things opened[21] which he desired to know, he caused all his nobility to come before his presence, before whom he caused to be brought

19 sped fared   **20 determined . . . go** determined that his soldiers should go   **21 opened** made manifest

the offenders also, and to them said: "Having thus conspired the death and destruction of me, which am the head
of the realm and governor of the people, it may be, no
doubt, but that you likewise have sworn the confusion of all
that are here with me and also the desolation of your own
country. To what horror (O Lord) for any true English heart
to consider, that such an execrable iniquity should ever so
bewrap you as, for pleasing of a foreign enemy, to imbrue
your hands in your blood and to ruin your own native soil!
Revenge herein touching my person though I seek not, yet
for the safeguard of you, my dear friends, and for due preservation of all sorts,²² I am by office to cause example
to be showed. Get ye hence, therefore, ye poor miserable
wretches, to the receiving of your just reward, wherein
God's majesty give you grace of his mercy and repentance
of your heinous offenses." And so immediately they were
had²³ to execution.

This done, the King, calling his lords again afore him,
said²⁴ in words few and with good grace. Of his enterprises
he recounted the honor and glory whereof they with him
were to be partakers; the great confidence he had in their
noble minds, which could not but remember them of ²⁵ the
famous feats that their ancestors aforetime in France had
achieved, whereof the due report forever recorded remained yet in register;²⁶ the great mercy of God that had so
graciously revealed unto him the treason at hand, whereby
the true hearts of those afore him made²⁷ so eminent and
apparent in his eye as they might be right sure he would
never forget it; the doubt²⁸ of danger to be nothing in respect of the certainty of honor that they should acquire,
wherein himself (as they saw) in person would be lord and
leader, through God's grace, to whose majesty, as chiefly
was known the equity of his demand,²⁹ even so to His mercy
did he only recommend the success of his travels.³⁰ When
the King had said, all the noblemen kneeled down and
promised faithfully to serve him, duly to obey him, and

---

22 sorts ranks   **23 had** taken   **24 said** spoke   **25 remember them of**
recall to their minds   **26 in register** in recorded history   **27 made** i.e.,
were made, or being made   **28 doubt** fear   **29 as chiefly . . . demand**
i.e., just as to God alone was fully known the justice of Henry's claim to
France   **30 travels** (with the idea also of *travails*, labors)

rather to die than to suffer him to fall into the hands of his enemies.

This done, the King thought that surely all treason and conspiracy had been utterly extinct, not suspecting the fire which was newly kindled and ceased not to increase till at length it burst out into such a flame that, catching the beams of his house and family, his line and stock was clean consumed to ashes. Divers[31] write that Richard, Earl of Cambridge, did not conspire with the Lord Scroop and Thomas Grey for the murdering of King Henry to please the French King withal, but only to the intent to exalt to the crown his brother-in-law Edmund, Earl of March, as heir to Lionel, Duke of Clarence; after the death of which Earl of March, for divers secret impediments not able to have issue, the Earl of Cambridge was sure that the crown should come to him by his wife and to his children of her begotten. And therefore, as was thought, he rather confessed himself for need of money to be corrupted by the French King than he would declare his inward mind and open his very intent and secret purpose which, if it were espied, he saw plainly that the Earl of March should have tasted of the same cup that he had drunken, and what should have come to his own children he much doubted.[32] Therefore, destitute of comfort and in despair of life, to save his children he feigned that tale, desiring rather to save his succession than himself, which he did indeed, for his son Richard, Duke of York, not privily but openly claimed the crown, and Edward his son both claimed it and gained it, as after it shall appear. . . .

But now to proceed with King Henry's doings. After this, when the wind came about prosperous to his purpose, he caused the mariners to weigh up anchors and hoise up sails and to set forward ships on the vigil of Our Lady Day the Assumption,[33] and took land at Caux, commonly called Kidcaux, where the river of Seine runneth into the sea, without resistance. At his first coming on land, he caused proclamation to be made that no person should be so hardy,[34] on pain of death, either to take anything out of any church that belonged to the same or to hurt or do any violence either to priests, women, or any such as should be

31 Divers various (authors) **32 doubted** feared **33 Our Lady Day the Assumption** 15 August **34 hardy** audacious found without weapon or armor and not ready to make resistance; also that no man should renew any quarrel or strife whereby any fray might arise to the disquieting of the army.

The next day after his landing, he marched toward the town of Harfleur, standing on the river of Seine between two hills. He besieged it on every side. . . .

The French King, being advertised that King Henry was arrived on that coast, sent in all haste the Lord Delabreth, Constable of France, the Seneschal of France, the Lord Boucicault, Marshal of France, the Seneschal of Hainault, the Lord Ligny, with other, which fortified towns with men, victuals, and artillery on all those frontiers towards the sea. And hearing that Harfleur was besieged, they came to the castle of Caudebec, being not far from Harfleur, to the intent they might succor their friends which were besieged by some policy or means. But the Englishmen, notwithstanding all the damage that that Frenchmen could work against them, forayed the country, spoiled the villages, bringing many a rich prey to the camp before Harfleur. And daily was the town assaulted, for the Duke of Gloucester, to whom the order of the seige was committed, made three mines under the ground and, approaching to the walls with his engines and ordnance,[35] would not suffer them within to take any rest.

For although they with their countermining somewhat disappointed the Englishmen and came to fight with them hand to hand within the mines so that they went no further forward with that work, yet they were so enclosed on each side, as well by water as land, that succor they saw could none come to them. . . .

The captains within the town, perceiving that they were not able long to resist the continual assaults of the Englishmen, knowing that their walls were undermined and like to be overthrown . . . at the first requested a truce until Sunday next following the feast of Saint Michael,[36] in which meantime, if no succor came to remove the siege, they would undertake to deliver the town into the King's hands, their lives and goods saved.

---

35 mines . . . engines and ordnance tunnels . . . catapults and artillery
36 feast of Saint Michael 29 September

The King advertised hereof, sent them word that, except they would surrender the town to him the morrow next ensuing without any condition, they should spend no more time in talk about the matter. But yet at length, through the earnest suit of the French lords, the King was contented to grant them truce until nine of the clock the next Sunday, being the two-and-twentieth of September, with condition that if in the meantime no rescue came, they should yield the town at that hour with their bodies and goods to stand at the King's pleasure. And for assurance thereof they delivered into the King's hands thirty of their best captains and merchants within that town as pledges.

[Since the Dauphin is unable to relieve the English siege of Harfleur, the town yields and is sacked by the English. Henry leaves Harfleur under the command of his uncle, the Duke of Exeter, and the Duke's lieutenant, one Sir John Falstaff.]

King Henry, after the winning of Harfleur, determined to have proceeded further in the winning of other towns and fortresses; but because the dead time of the winter approached, it was determined by advice of his Council that he should in all convenient speed set forward and march through the country towards Calais by land, lest his return as then homewards should of slanderous tongues be named a running away. And yet that journey was adjudged perilous by reason that the number of his people was much minished[37] by the flux[38]* and other fevers which sore vexed and brought to death above fifteen hundred persons of the army; and this was the cause that his return was the sooner appointed and concluded.

[Henry deals mercifully with his French prisoners in Harfleur, rebuilds the town's fortifications, and heads for Calais. The French destroy crops in advance of Henry's army and harass him with skirmishes. Henry crosses the Somme.]

[He] determined to make haste towards Calais and not to

37 minished diminished   **38 flux** dysentery

seek for battle except he were thereto constrained, because that[39] his army by sickness was sore diminished, insomuch that he had but only two thousand horsemen and thirteen thousand archers, billmen,[40] and of all sorts of other footmen.

The Englishmen were brought into some distress in this journey by reason of their victuals in manner spent and no hope to get more, for the enemies had destroyed all the corn[41] before they came. Rest could they none take, for their enemies with alarms[42] did ever so infest them. Daily it rained and nightly it freezed; of fuel there was great scarcity, of fluxes plenty; money enough, but wares for their relief to bestow it on had they none. Yet in this great necessity the poor people of the country were not spoiled,[43] nor anything taken of them without payment nor any outrage or offense done by the Englishmen except one, which was that a soldier took a pyx[44] out of a church, for which he was apprehended, and the King not once removed till the box was restored and the offender strangled. The people of the countries thereabout, hearing of such zeal in him to the maintenance of justice, ministered to his army victuals and other necessaries, although by open proclamation so to do they were prohibited.

The French King being at Rouen, and hearing that King Henry was passed the river of Somme, was much displeased therewith and, assembling his council to the number of five-and-thirty, asked their advice what was to be done. There was amongst these five-and-thirty his son the Dauphin, calling himself King of Sicily, the Dukes of Berri and Brittany, the Earl of Pontrieux* (the King's youngest son), and other high estates.[45] At length thirty of them agreed that the Englishmen should not depart unfought withal, and five were of a contrary opinion; but the greater number ruled the matter. And so Montjoy, King-at-Arms,[46] was sent to the King of England to defy him as the enemy of

---

39 because that because   **40 billmen** soldiers armed with halberds
41 corn grain   **42 alarms** alarums, surprise attacks   **43 spoiled** plundered   **44 pyx** vessel containing the consecrated host in the Mass. (But see *Henry V*, 3.6.40 and note, where Bardolph is reported to have stolen a *pax*, or metal disk stamped with the crucifix, employed in the Mass.)
45 estates ranks   **46 King-at-Arms** chief herald

France and to tell him that he should shortly have battle. King Henry advisedly answered: "Mine intent is to do as it pleaseth God. I will not seek your master at this time, but if he or his seek me, I will meet with them, God willing. If any of your nation attempt once to stop me in my journey now towards Calais, at their jeopardy be it; and yet wish I not any of you so unadvised as to be the occasion that I dye your tawny ground with your red blood."

When he had thus answered the herald, he gave him a princely reward and license to depart. Upon whose return with this answer, it was incontinently[47] on the French side proclaimed that all men-of-war should resort to the Constable to fight with the King of England. Whereupon all men apt for armor and desirous of honor drew them toward the field. The Dauphin sore desired to have been at the battle, but he was prohibited by his father.

[King Henry, "without all fear or trouble of mind," rides forth unaccompanied by his soldiers to view the French army. Returning to his troops "with cheerful countenance," he puts them in order of battle. The English are unfamiliar with the terrain.]

There was not one amongst them that knew any certain place whither to go in that unknown country, but by chance they happened upon a beaten way, white in sight,[48] by the which they were brought unto a little village where they were refreshed with meat and drink somewhat more plenteously than they had been divers days before. Order was taken by commandment from the King, after the army was first set in battle array, that no noise or clamor should be made in the host, so that in marching forth to this village every man kept himself quiet. But at their coming into the village, fires were made to give light on every side, as there likewise were in the French host, which was encamped not past two hundred and fifty paces distant from the English. The chief leaders of the French host were these: the Constable of France, the Marshal,[49] the Admiral,[50] the Lord Rambures, Master of the Crossbows, and other of the French

47 incontinently immediately   **48 sight** appearance   **49 the Marshal** i.e., Lord Boucicault   **50 the Admiral** i.e., Lord Châtillon

nobility, which came and pitched down their standards and banners in the county of Saint Paul, within the territory of Agincourt, having in their army, as some write, to the number of threescore thousand horsemen, besides footmen, wagoners, and other.

They were lodged even in the way by the which the Englishmen must needs pass towards Calais; and all that night, after their coming thither, made great cheer and were very merry, pleasant, and full of game. The Englishmen also for their parts were of good comfort and nothing abashed of the matter, and yet they were both hungry, weary, sore traveled, and vexed with many cold diseases. Howbeit, reconciling themselves with God by housel and shrift,[51] requiring[52] assistance at his hands that is the only giver of victory, they determined rather to die than to yield or flee. The day following was the five-and-twentieth of October in the year 1415, being then Friday and the feast of Crispin and Crispinian, a day fair and fortunate to the English but most sorrowful and unlucky to the French.

[The French army is reckoned to outnumber the English army six to one. Both armies are deployed for battle by their leaders. King Henry assigns to Edward, Duke of York, the leading of the vanguard.]

Thus the King, having ordered his battles,[53] feared not the puissance of his enemies. But yet to provide that they should not with the multitude of horsemen break the order of his archers, in whom the force of his army consisted (for in those days the yeomen had their limbs at liberty, sith their hosen were then fastened with one point,[54] and their jacks[55] long and easy to shoot in, so that they might draw bows of great strength and shoot arrows of a yard long, beside the head), he caused stakes bound with iron sharp at both ends, of the length of five or six foot, to be pitched before the archers and of each side the footmen like an hedge,

---

51 **housel and shrift** the Mass and confession   52 **requiring** begging
53 **battles** battalions, troops   54 **point** tagged lace for attaching lower
to upper garment   55 **jacks** sleeveless long coats, often mailed

to the intent that if the barded[56] horses ran rashly upon
them they might shortly be gored and destroyed. Certain
persons also were appointed to remove the stakes, as by the
moving of the archers occasion and time should require, so
that the footmen were hedged about with stakes and the
horsemen stood like a bulwark between them and their enemies without the stakes. . . .

King Henry, by reason of his small number of people to
fill up his battles, placed his vanguard so on the right hand
of the main battle, which himself led, that the distance betwixt them might scarce be perceived, and so in like case
was the rearward[57] joined on the left hand, that the one
might the more readily succor another in time of need.
When he had thus ordered his battles he left a small company to keep his camp and carriage, which remained still in
the village, and then, calling his captains and soldiers
about him, he made to them a right grave oration, moving
them to play the men whereby to obtain a glorious victory,
as there was hope certain they should, the rather if they
would but remember the just cause for which they fought
and whom they should encounter—such fainthearted people as their ancestors had so often overcome. To conclude,
many words of courage he uttered to stir them to do manfully, assuring them that England should never be charged
with his ransom nor any Frenchman triumph over him as a
captive, for either by famous death or glorious victory
would he, by God's grace, win honor and fame.

It is said that, as he heard one of the host utter his wish to
another thus, "I would to God there were with us now so
many good soldiers as are at this hour within England!" the
King answered: "I would not wish a man more here than I
have. We are indeed in comparison to the enemies but a few,
but if God of his clemency do favor us and our just cause, as
I trust He will, we shall speed well enough. But let no man
ascribe victory to our own strength and might, but only to
God's assistance, to whom I have no doubt we shall worthily have cause to give thanks therefor. And if so be that
for our offenses' sakes we shall be delivered into the hands

56 barded caparisoned, with ornamental cloths covering saddle or
harness   **57 rearward** rearguard

of our enemies, the less number we be, the less damage shall the realm of England sustain; but if we should fight in trust of multitude of men and so get the victory, our minds being prone to pride, we should thereupon peradventure ascribe the victory not so much to the gift of God as to our own puissance and thereby provoke his high indignation and displeasure against us; and if the enemy get the upper hand, then should our realm and country suffer more damage and stand in further danger. But be you of good comfort[58] and show yourselves valiant, God and our just quarrel[59] shall defend us and deliver these our proud adversaries with all the multitude of them which you see, or at the least the most of them, into our hands." Whilst the King was yet thus in speech, either army so maligned the other, being as then in open sight, that every man cried "Forward, forward!" The Dukes of Clarence, Gloucester, and York were of the same opinion, yet the King stayed a while lest any jeopardy were not foreseen or any hazard not prevented. The Frenchmen in the meanwhile, as though they had been sure of victory, made great triumph, for the captains had determined before how to divide the spoil, and the soldiers the night before had played[60] the Englishmen at dice. The noblemen had devised a chariot wherein they might triumphantly convey the King captive to the city of Paris, crying to their soldiers, "Haste you to the spoil,[61] glory, and honor!"—little weening[62] (God wot) how soon their brags should be blown away.

Here we may not forget how the French, thus in their jollity, sent an herald to King Henry to inquire what ransom he would offer. Whereunto he answered that within two or three hours he hoped it would so happen that the Frenchmen should be glad to commune[63] rather with the Englishmen for their ransoms than the English to take thought for their deliverance, promising for his own part that his dead carcass should rather be a prize to the Frenchmen than that his living body should pay any ransom. When the messenger was come back to the French host, the men-of-war put on their helmets and caused their trumpets to

---

58 **But . . . comfort** but if you take comfort (in the justice of the cause)
59 **quarrel** cause 60 **played** gambled for 61 **spoil** plundering
62 **weening** believing, imagining 63 **commune** confer, communicate

blow to the battle. They thought themselves so sure of victory that divers of the noblemen made such haste towards the battle that they left many of their servants and men-of-war behind them, and some of them would not once stay for their standards; as, amongst other, the Duke of Brabant, when his standard was not come, caused a banner to be taken from a trumpet and fastened to a spear, the which he commanded to be borne before him instead of his standard.

[The armies face each other in full order of battle and join in combat. The English throw the French into serious confusion, first with their archery and then in hand-to-hand combat.]

The King that day showed himself a valiant knight, albeit almost felled by the Duke of Alençon; yet with plain strength he slew two of the Duke's company and felled the Duke himself, whom, when he would have yielded, the King's guard (contrary to his mind)[64] slew out of hand. In conclusion, the King, minding[65] to make an end of that day's journey,[66] caused his horsemen to fetch a compass about[67] and to join with him against the rearward of the Frenchmen, in the which was the greatest number of people. When the Frenchmen perceived his intent, they were suddenly amazed and ran away like sheep, without order or array. Which when the King perceived, he encouraged his men and followed so quickly upon the enemies that they ran hither and thither, casting away their armor; many on their knees desired to have their lives saved.

In the mean season, while the battle thus continued and that the Englishmen had taken a great number of prisoners, certain Frenchmen on horseback . . . to the number of six hundred horsemen, which were the first that fled, hearing that the English tents and pavilions were a good way distant from the army without any sufficient guard to defend the same, either upon a covetous meaning to gain by the spoil or upon a desire to be revenged, entered upon the King's

---

64 to his mind i.e., to the King's wishes   **65 minding** intending
66 journey i.e., battle, day's work   **67 fetch a compass about** reverse
course

camp and there spoiled the hales,[68] robbed the tents, brake
up chests and carried away caskets, and slew such servants
as they found to make any resistance. For which treason
and haskardy[69] in thus leaving their camp at the very point
of fight, for winning of spoil where none to defend it, very
many were after committed to prison and had lost their
lives if the Dauphin had longer lived.

But when the outcry of the lackeys and boys, which ran
away for fear of the Frenchmen thus spoiling the camp,
came to the King's ears, he, doubting[70] lest his enemies
should gather together again and begin a new field,[71] and
mistrusting further that the prisoners would be an aid to
his enemies or the very enemies to their takers indeed if
they were suffered to live, contrary to his accustomed gen-
tleness commanded by sound of trumpet that every man
upon pain of death should incontinently[72] slay his prisoner.
When this dolorous decree and pitiful proclamation was
pronounced, pity it was to see how some Frenchmen were
suddenly sticked with daggers, some were brained with
poleaxes, some slain with mauls,[73] other had their throats
cut, and some their bellies paunched,[74] so that in effect, having respect to the great number,[75] few prisoners were saved.

When this lamentable slaughter was ended, the Englishmen disposed themselves in order of battle, ready to abide a
new field and also to invade and newly set on their enemies.
With great force they assailed the Earls of Marle and
Faulconbridge and the Lords of Lorraine* and of Thines,*
with six hundred men-of-arms, who had all that day kept
together but now slain and beaten down out of hand. Some
write that the King, perceiving his enemies in one part[76] to
assemble together as though they meant to give a new battle for preservation of the prisoners, sent to them an herald,
commanding them either to depart out of his sight or else
to come forward at once and give battle, promising here-
with that if they did offer to fight again, not only those prisoners which his people already had taken but also so many

---

68 spoiled the hales plundered the pavilions, temporary shelters
69 haskardy baseness   **70 doubting** fearing   **71 field** battle   **72 incontinently** immediately   **73 mauls** maces   **74 paunched** stabbed   **75 having . . . number** in relation to the large number there were   **76 part** part
of the field

of them as in this new conflict which they thus attempted should fall into his hands should die the death without redemption.

The Frenchmen, fearing the sentence of so terrible a decree, without further delay parted out of the field. And so, about four of the clock in the afternoon, the King, when he saw no appearance of enemies, caused the retreat[77] to be blown and, gathering his army together, gave thanks to almighty God for so happy a victory, causing his prelates and chaplains to sing this psalm: *"In exitu Israel de Aegypto,"*[78] and commanded every man to kneel down on the ground at this verse: *"Non nobis, Domine, non nobis, sed nomini tuo da gloriam."*[79] Which done, he caused *"Te Deum"*[80] with certain anthems to be sung, giving laud and praise to God without boasting of his own force or any human power. That night he and his people took rest and refreshed themselves with such victuals as they found in the French camp, but lodged in the same village where he lay the night before.

In the morning, Montjoy, King-at-Arms, and four other French heralds came to the King to know the number of prisoners and to desire burial for the dead. Before he made them answer, to understand what they would say he demanded of them why they made to him that request, considering that he knew not whether the victory was his or theirs. When Montjoy by true and just confession had cleared that doubt to the high praise of the King, he desired of Montjoy to understand the name of the castle near adjoining. When they had told him that it was called Agincourt, he said, "Then shall this conflict be called the Battle of Agincourt." He feasted the French officers-of-arms that day and granted them their request, which busily sought through the field for such as were slain. But the Englishmen suffered them not to go alone, for they searched with them and found many hurt but not in jeopardy of their lives, whom they took prisoners and brought them to their tents. When the King of England had well refreshed himself and

---

77 retreat signal to cease fighting (not to retreat before the enemy)
78 In exitu . . . Aegypto When Israel went out of Egypt. (Psalm 114.)
79 Non nobis . . . gloriam Not unto us, O Lord, not unto us, but unto thy name give glory. (Psalm 115.) **80 Te Deum** We thank thee O God. (A hymn of thanksgiving.)

his soldiers that had taken the spoil of such as were slain, he with his prisoners in good order returned to his town of Calais.

When tidings of this great victory was blown into England, solemn processions and other praisings to almighty God with bonfires and joyful triumphs were ordained in every town, city, and borough, and the Mayor and citizens of London went the morrow after the day of Saint Simon and Jude from the church of Saint Paul to the church of Saint Peter at Westminster in devout manner, rendering to God hearty thanks for such fortunate luck sent to the King and his army. The same Sunday that the King removed from the camp at Agincourt towards Calais, divers Frenchmen came to the field to view again the dead bodies . . . wherein [eventually] were buried by account five thousand and eight hundred persons, besides them that were carried away by their friends and servants and others which, being wounded, died in hospitals and other places.

After this their dolorous journey and pitiful slaughter, divers clerks of Paris made many a lamentable verse, complaining that the King reigned by will and that councillors were partial, affirming that the noblemen fled against nature and that the commons were destroyed by their prodigality, declaring also that the clergy were dumb and durst not say the truth and that the humble commons duly obeyed and yet ever suffered punishment, for which cause by divine persecution the less number vanquished the greater. Wherefore they concluded that all things went out of order, and yet was there no man that studied to bring the unruly to frame. It was no marvel though this battle was lamentable to the French nation, for in it were taken and slain the flower of all the nobility of France.

There were taken prisoners Charles, Duke of Orleans, nephew to the French King; John, Duke of Bourbon; the Lord Boucicault, one of the Marshals of France (he after died in England); with a number of other lords, knights, and esquires, at the least fifteen hundred, besides the common people. There were slain in all of the French part to the number of ten thousand men, whereof were princes and noblemen bearing banners one hundred twenty-and-six; to these, of knights, esquires, and gentlemen, so many as made up the number of eight thousand and four hundred (of the which five hundred were dubbed knights the night before the battle); so as of the meaner[81] sort, not past sixteen hundred. Amongst those of the nobility that were slain, these were the chiefest: Charles, Lord Delabreth, High Constable of France; Jacques of Châtillon, Lord of Dampierre, Admiral of France; the Lord Rambures, Master of the Crossbows; Sir Guichard Dauphin, Great Master of France; John, Duke of Alençon; Anthony, Duke of Brabant, brother to the Duke of Burgundy; Edward, Duke of Bar; the Earl of Nevers, another brother to the Duke of Burgundy; with the Earls of Marle, Vaudemont, Beaumont, Grandpré, Roussi, Faulconbridge, Foix, and Lestrale,* besides a great number of lords and barons of name.

Of Englishmen, there died at this battle Edward, Duke of York; the Earl of Suffolk; Sir Richard Ketly* and Davy Gam, Esquire; and of all other not above five-and-twenty persons, as some do report; but other writers of greater credit affirm that there were slain above five or six hundred persons. Titus Livius[82] saith that there were slain of Englishmen, besides the Duke of York and the Earl of Suffolk, an hundred persons at the first encounter. The Duke of Gloucester, the King's brother, was sore wounded about the hips and borne down to the ground so that he fell backwards, with his feet towards his enemies, whom the King bestrid and like a brother valiantly rescued from his enemies and, so saving his life, caused him to be conveyed out of the fight into a place of more safety. . . .

After that the King of England had refreshed himself and his people at Calais, and that such prisoners as he had left at Harfleur (as ye have heard) were come to Calais unto him, the sixth day of November he with all his prisoners took shipping. . . . The Mayor of London and the aldermen, appareled in orient-grained scarlet,[83] and four hundred commoners clad in beautiful murrey,[84] well mounted and trimly horsed, with rich collars and great chains, met the King on Blackheath, rejoicing at his return. And the clergy of London, with rich crosses, sumptuous copes, and massy cen-

---

81 meaner of lower station   **82 Titus Livius** author of the *Vita Henrici Quinti* (c. 1437), an early biography of Henry V   **83 orient-grained scarlet** a lustrous dyed scarlet cloth   **84 murrey** cloth of purple-red mulberry color

sers, received him at Saint Thomas of Waterings with
solemn procession.

The King, like a grave and sober personage and as one
remembering from whom all victories are sent, seemed little to regard such vain pomp and shows as were in triumphant sort devised for his welcoming home from so
prosperous a journey, insomuch that he would not suffer
his helmet to be carried with him, whereby might have appeared to the people the blows and dints that were to be
seen in the same; neither would he suffer any ditties to be
made and sung by minstrels of his glorious victory, for that
he would wholly have the praise and thanks altogether
given to God. The news of this bloody battle being reported
to the French King as then sojourning at Rouen filled the
court full of sorrow.

[The Dauphin dies soon after Agincourt, either of melan-
choly or of some sudden disease. In 1415 the English continue further their successful campaigning in France,
meanwhile forging a league with the Emperor Sigismund
and signing a truce with the Duke of Burgundy. In 1417
Henry again campaigns in France and takes Caen. The
Scots are successfully repulsed in the north of England. In
1418 Henry captures Cherbourg and lays down a siege before Rouen, causing extreme suffering and hunger within
the city. Early in 1419, the King, still at the seige of Rouen,
agrees to receive a French delegation requesting a parley.]

One of them, seen[85] in the civil laws, was appointed to declare the message in all their names, who, showing himself
more rash than wise, more arrogant than learned, first took
upon him to show wherein the glory of victory consisted,
advising the King not to show his manhood in famishing a
multitude of poor, simple, and innocent people but rather
suffer such miserable wretches as lay betwixt the walls of
the city and the trenches of his siege to pass through the
camp, that they might get their living in other places, and
then, if he durst manfully assault the city and by force sub-
due it, he should win both worldly fame and merit great

85 seen well versed, learned

meed[86] at the hands of almighty God for having compassion of the poor, needy, and indigent people.

When this orator had said,[87] the King, who no request less suspected than that which was thus desired,[88] began awhile to muse; and after he had well considered the crafty cautel[89] of his enemies, with a fierce countenance and bold spirit he reproved them both for their subtle dealing with him and their malapert presumption in that they should seem to go about to teach him what belonged to the duty of a conqueror. And therefore since it appeared that the same was unknown unto them, he declared that the goddess of battle, called Bellona, had three handmaidens ever of necessity attending upon her, as blood, fire, and famine. And whereas it lay in his choice to use them all three—yea, two or one of them, at his pleasure—he had appointed only the meekest maid[90] of those three damsels to punish them of that city till they were brought to reason.

And whereas the gain of a captain attained by any of the said three handmaidens was both glorious, honorable, and worthy of triumph, yet of all the three, the youngest maid, which he meant to use at that time, was most profitable and commodious. And as for the poor people lying in the ditches, if they died through famine, the fault was theirs that like cruel tyrants had put them out of the town to the intent he should slay them; and yet he had saved their lives, so that if any lack of charity was, it rested in them and not in him. But to their cloaked request,[91] he meant not to gratify them within so much, but they should keep them still to help to spend their victuals.[92] And as to assault the town, he told them that he would they should know he was both able and willing thereto, as he should see occasion; but the choice was in his hand to tame them either with blood, fire, or famine, or with them all, whereof he would take the choice at his pleasure and not at theirs.

86 meed reward   **87 said** finished speaking   **88 who . . . desired** who would have expected just about any request sooner than this one **89 cautel** device   **90 the meekest maid** i.e., famine   **91 cloaked request** i.e., a cunning request cloaked as a seemingly innocent one   **92 but they . . . victuals** i.e., Henry will insist on their keeping all the poor etc. who depend on the city to be fed in order that Rouen's supplies will be the more quickly exhausted

[Rouen surrenders. After further campaigning, the Duke of Burgundy sends letters and ambassadors to King Henry urging a meeting between him and Charles, the French King. A place is arranged for the negotiations.]

The place of interview and meeting was appointed to be beside Meulan on the river of Seine, where in a fair place every part was by commissioners appointed to their ground. When the day of appointment approached, which was the last day of May, the King of England, accompanied with the Dukes of Clarence and Gloucester, his brethren, the Duke of Exeter, his uncle, and Henry Beaufort, clerk,[93] his other uncle, which after was Bishop of Winchester and Cardinal, with the Earls of March, Salisbury, and others, to the number of a thousand men-of-war, entered into his ground, which was barred about and ported, wherein his tents were pight[94] in a princely manner.

Likewise for the French part came Isabel, the French Queen, because her husband was fallen into his old frantic disease, having in her company the Duke of Burgundy and the Earl of Saint Paul, and she had attending upon her the fair Lady Katharine her daughter, with six-and-twenty ladies and damosels; and had also for her furniture a thousand men-of-war. The said Lady Katharine was brought by her mother only to the intent that the King of England, beholding her excellent beauty, should be so inflamed and rapt in her love that he, to obtain her to his wife, should the sooner agree to a gentle peace and loving concord. But though many words were spent in this treaty and that they met at eight several times, yet no effect ensued, nor any conclusion was taken by this friendly consultation, so that both parties after a princely fashion took leave each of other and departed, the Englishmen to Mantes and the Frenchmen to Pontoise.

[The negotiations appear to be making slight progress, "save only that a certain spark of burning love was kindled in the King's heart by the sight of the Lady Katharine." Negotiations break off, and before they can be resumed more

93 clerk cleric   **94 ported . . . pight** gated . . . pitched

fighting takes place. Pontoise and Gisors fall to King Henry, then all of Burgundy. When the Duke of Burgundy is murdered by the Dauphin's followers, his son Philip takes up the cause of urging peace.]

Whilst these victorious exploits were thus happily achieved by the Englishmen, and that the King lay still at Rouen in giving thanks to almighty God for the same, there came to him eftsoons[95] ambassadors from the French King and the Duke of Burgundy to move him to peace. The King, minding[96] not to be reputed for a destroyer of the country which he coveted to preserve, or for a causer of Christian blood still to be spilt in his quarrel, began so to incline and give ear unto their suit and humble request that at length, after often sending to and fro, and that the Bishop of Arras and other men of honor had been with him, and likewise the Earl of Warwick and the Bishop of Rochester had been with the Duke of Burgundy, they both finally agreed upon certain articles, so[97] that the French King and his commons would thereto assent.

Now was the French King and the Queen with their daughter, Katharine, at Troyes in Champagne governed and ordered by them, which so much favored the Duke of Burgundy that they would not, for any earthly good, once hinder or pull back one jot of such articles as the same Duke should seek to prefer. And therefore what needeth many words? A truce tripartite was accorded between the two Kings and the Duke and their countries, and order taken that the King of England should send, in the company of the Duke of Burgundy, his ambassadors unto Troyes in Champagne, sufficiently authorized to treat and conclude of so great matter. The King of England, being in good hope that all his affairs should take good success as he could wish or desire, sent to the Duke of Burgundy his uncle, the Duke of Exeter, the Earl of Salisbury, the Bishop of Ely, the Lord Fanhope, the Lord Fitzhugh, Sir John Robsert, and Sir Philip Hall, with divers doctors[98] to the number of five hundred horse, which in the company of the Duke of Burgundy

95 eftsoons again   **96 minding** wishing, intending   **97 so** provided
98 doctors i.e., doctors of divinity and law

came to the city of Troyes the eleventh of March [1420]. The
King, the Queen, and the Lady Katharine them received and
heartily welcomed, showing great signs and tokens of love
and amity.

After a few days they fell to council, in which at length it
was concluded that King Henry of England should come to
Troyes and marry the Lady Katharine, and the King her
father after his death should make him heir of his realm,
crown, and dignity. It was also agreed that King Henry, during his father-in-law's life, should in his stead have the
whole government of the realm of France, as Regent
thereof, with many other covenants and articles, as after
shall appear. To the performance whereof it was accorded
that all the nobles and estates of the realm of France, as
well spiritual as temporal, and also the cities and common-
alties, citizens, and burgesses of towns that were obeisant
at that time to the French King, should take a corporal
oath.[99] These articles were not at the first in all points
brought to a perfect conclusion. But after the effect and
meaning of them was agreed upon by the commissioners,
the Englishmen departed towards the King their master
and left Sir John Robsert behind to give his attendance on
the Lady Katharine.

[King Henry agrees to the meeting at Troyes.]

The Duke of Burgundy, accompanied with many noblemen, received him two leagues without[100] the town and conveyed him to his lodging. All his army was lodged in small
villages thereabout. And after that he had reposed himself
a little, he went to visit the French King, the Queen, and the
Lady Katharine, whom he found in Saint Peter's church,
where was a very joyous meeting betwixt them (and this
was on the twentieth day of May), and there the King of England and the Lady Katharine were affianced. After this the
two Kings and their council assembled together divers
days, wherein the first concluded agreement was in divers
points altered and brought to a certainty according to the
effect above mentioned.

---

99 obeisant . . . corporal oath obedient . . . oath ratified by touching a
sacred object   **100 without** outside of

[The marriage between King Henry and the Lady Katharine is solemnized on the third of June, 1420, and Henry is proclaimed heir and Regent of France. The articles of peace include the following:]

1. First, it is accorded between our father and us that forsomuch as by the bond of matrimony made for the good of the peace between us and our most dear beloved Katharine, daughter of our said father and of our most dear mother Isabel, his wife, the same Charles and Isabel been made[101] our father and mother, therefore them as our father and mother we shall have and worship, as it fitteth and seemeth so worthy a prince and princess to be worshiped, principally before all other temporal persons of the world. . . .

6. Also, that after the death of our said father aforesaid, and from thenceforward, the crown and the realm of France, with all the rights and appurtenances, shall remain and abide to us, and been of us and of our heirs forevermore.

7. And forsomuch as our said father is withholden with[102] divers sickness, in such manner as he may not intend[103] in his own person for to[104] dispose for the needs of the foresaid realm of France, therefore during the life of our foresaid father, the faculties and exercise of the governance and disposition of the public and common profit of the said realm of France, with Council and nobles and wise men of the same realm of France, shall be and abide to us. . . .

24. Also, that during our father's life we shall not call nor write us King of France; but verily we shall abstain us from that name as long as our father liveth.

25. Also, that our said father, during his life, shall name, call, and write us in French in this manner: *"Notre très cher fils, Henri, Roi d'Angleterre, Héritier de France,"* and in Latin in this manner: *Praeclarissimus filius noster Henricus, Rex Angliae et Haeres Franciae."* . . .

28. Also that thenceforward, perpetually, shall be still

---

101 been made have been made (by the marriage)   **102 withholden with** i.e., kept from the performance of his duties by   **103 intend** direct his attention, pay heed   **104 for to** to rest,[105] and that in all manner of wise, dissensions, hates, rancors, envies, and wars between the same realms of France and England and the people of the same realms, drawing to accord of the same peace, may cease and be broken.

[King Henry subsequently dies on campaign in France in April 1422. Holinshed gives a view of his character.]

This Henry was a king, of life without spot; a prince whom all men loved and of none disdained; a captain against whom fortune never frowned nor mischance once spurned; whose people him, so severe a justicer, both loved and obeyed, and so humane withal that he left no offense unpunished nor friendship unrewarded;[106] a terror to rebels and suppressor of sedition; his virtues notable, his qualities most praiseworthy.

In strength and nimbleness of body from his youth few to him comparable, for in wrestling, leaping, and running no man well able to compare. In casting of great iron bars and heavy stones he excelled commonly all men, never shrinking at cold nor slothful for heat; and when he most labored, his head commonly uncovered; no more weary of harness[107] than a light cloak; very valiantly abiding at needs[108] both hunger and thirst; so manful of mind as never seen to qunich[109] at a wound or to smart at the pain, not to turn his nose from evil savor nor close his eyes from smoke or dust; no man more moderate in eating and drinking, with diet not delicate but rather more meet for men-of-war than for princes or tender stomachs. Every honest person was permitted to come to him, sitting at meal, where, either secretly or openly, to declare his mind. High and weighty causes, as well between men-of-war and other, he would gladly hear, and either determined them himself or else for end[110] committed them to others. He slept very little, but

---

105 still rest continual peace **106 whose people . . . unrewarded** i.e., whose people both obeyed and loved him, obeying the severe judge who left no offense unpunished and loving the humane man who left no friendship unrewarded **107 harness** armor **108 abiding at needs** enduring when necessary **109 qunich** flinch **110 for end** for a final determination

that very soundly, insomuch that when his soldiers sung at nights or minstrels played he then slept fastest; of courage invincible; of purpose unmutable; so wisehardy[111] always as[112] fear was banished from him; at every alarum he first in armor and foremost in ordering. In time of war such was his providence, bounty, and hap as[113] he had true intelligence not only what his enemies did but what they said and intended; of his devises and purposes few, before the thing was at the point to be done should be made privy.[114]

He had such knowledge in ordering and guiding an army, with such a gift to encourage his people, that the Frenchmen had constant opinion he could never be vanquished in battle. Such wit, such prudence, and such policy[115] withal that he never enterprised anything before he had fully debated and forecast all the main chances that might happen, which done, with all diligence and courage he set his purpose forward. What policy he had in finding present remedies for sudden mischiefs and what engines[116] in saving himself and his people in sharp distresses, were it not that by his acts they did plainly appear, hard were it by words to make them credible. Wantonness of life and thirst in avarice had he quite quenched in him; virtues indeed in such an estate of sovereignty, youth, and power, as very rare, so right commendable in the highest degree. So staid of mind and countenance besides that never jolly or triumphant for victory nor sad or damped for loss or misfortune. For bountifulness and liberality, no man more free, gentle, and frank[117] in bestowing rewards to all persons according to their deserts; for his saying was that he never desired money to keep but to give and spend.

Although that story[118] properly serves not for theme of praise or dispraise, yet what in brevity may well be remembered, in truth would not be forgotten by sloth,[119] were it but only to remain as a spectacle for magnanimity to have al-

---

111 wisehardy intelligently brave (the opposite of foolhardy)   **112 as** that   **113 providence, bounty, and hap as** foresight, warlike prowess, and good luck that   **114 of his devices ... privy** i.e., he was careful that plans were kept secret and known to few until the time was ready for those plans to be executed   **115 policy** stratagem   **116 engines** clever devices   **117 frank** openhanded   **118 Although that story** although history   **119 yet what ... sloth** yet whatever can be only briefly recorded here truly should not be slothfully forgotten

ways in eye and for encouragement to nobles in honorable
enterprises. Known be it therefore, of person and form was
this prince rightly representing his heroical affects:[120] of
stature and proportion tall and manly, rather lean than
gross, somewhat long-necked and black-haired, of countenance amiable. Eloquent and grave was his speech, and of
great grace and power to persuade. For conclusion, a majesty was he that both lived and died a pattern in prince-
hood, a lodestar[121] in honor, and mirror of magnificence; the
more highly exalted in his life, the more deeply lamented at
his death and famous to the world alway.

The second edition of Raphael Holinshed's *Chronicles* was published in
1587. This selection is based on that edition, Volume 3, Folios 545–583.

In the following, departures from the original text appear in boldface; original readings are in roman.

p. 128 *Kenilworth Killingworth   **p. 133 *he** [not in 1587 ed.]   **p. 137 *flux** flix
p. 138 *Pontrieux Pontieu   **p. 144 *Lorraine** Louraie   ***Thines** Thine   **p. 147 *Faulconbridge, Foix, and Lestrale** Fauconberge, Fois and Lestrake   **p. 147 *Ketly** Kikelie

120 of person . . . affects the person and shape of this prince truly
reflected his heroical disposition   **121 lodestar** guiding star, especially
the North Pole star

Further Reading

Beauman, Sally, ed. *The Royal Shakespeare Company's Production of "Henry V" for the Centenary Season at the Royal Shakespeare Theatre*. Oxford: Pergamon Press, 1976. Beauman provides a record of the development of the Royal Shakespeare Company's 1975 production of *Henry V*. The working script, an introduction by director Terry Hands, interviews with the cast, and selections from the London drama critics are combined in a volume that is at once a portrait of a production and an unusual and powerful piece of literary criticism.

Berman, Ronald, ed. *Twentieth Century Interpretations of "Henry V."* Englewood Cliffs, N.J.: Prentice-Hall, 1968. Berman offers a useful selection of extracts and critical essays on the play, including commentary by William Butler Yeats, A. C. Bradley, J. Dover Wilson, E. M. W. Tillyard, and A. P. Rossiter.

Berry, Ralph. *"Henry V." Changing Styles in Shakespeare.* London: George Allen and Unwin, 1981. Berry studies recent changes in the dramatic presentation of *Henry V* as they reflect significant shifts in the understanding of the play. Focusing on Laurence Olivier's film (1944), two Canadian productions by Michael Langham, and two Royal Shakespeare Company productions, Peter Hall's (1964) and Terry Hands's (1975), Berry shows how performance reflects "current social assumptions and preoccupations."

Calderwood, James L. *"Henry V: The Art of Order." Metadrama in Shakespeare's Henriad: "Richard II" to "Henry V."* Berkeley and Los Angeles: Univ. of California Press, 1979. Calderwood explores the principles of order that the play presents. National unity and artistic unity are seen as parallel achievements, each accomplished by parts being subordinated to the whole. The process is visible even in the character of the King, as Henry's personal life disappears, subordinated to the necessities of rule.

Campbell, Lily B. "The Victorious Acts of King Henry V." *Shakespeare's "Histories": Mirrors of Elizabethan Policy.*

San Marino, Calif.: Huntington Library, 1947. For Campbell, *Henry V* is an epic celebration of the English "achieving victory through the blessing of God." Shakespeare portrays Henry as an "ideal hero," whose thoughts and actions are seen by Campbell to be based on Elizabethan theories of warfare.

Dollimore, Jonathan, and Alan Sinfield. "History and Ideology: The Instance of *Henry V*." In *Alternative Shakespeares*, ed. John Drakakis. London and New York: Methuen, 1985. Dollimore and Sinfield examine the play's representation of power in the context of "the struggles of its own historical moment." They see Henry's effort to conquer France "as a re-presentation of [Elizabeth's] attempt to conquer Ireland and the hoped-for unity of Britain," and focus on the social conflicts and contradictions that the play, a fantasy of national unity, would deny.

Goldman, Michael. "*Henry V:* The Strain of Rule." *Shakespeare and the Energies of Drama*. Princeton, N.J.: Princeton Univ. Press, 1972. Goldman explores the play's focus on "the effort of greatness," the strain under which Henry places himself and his hearers. The play recognizes both the "glory of the ruler" and "the price of his role," and yet "with all its ironies it remains great patriotic drama."

Goddard, Harold C. "*Henry V*." *The Meaning of Shakespeare*. Chicago: Univ. of Chicago Press, 1951. Goddard finds the play colored by a pervasive irony that disrupts the celebration of Henry's role. The Chorus, Goddard finds, voices the popular conception of England's famous hero-king, but in the action and the parodic subplot Shakespeare "tells the truth about him": he is a brutal "Machiavellian prince."

Hazlitt, William. "*Henry V*." *Characters of Shakespear's Plays*, 1817. Rpt., London: Oxford Univ. Press, 1966. Hazlitt offers the first influential attack on the character of Henry. Hazlitt finds him "careless, dissolute and ambitious," and he argues that "he seemed to have no idea of any rule of right or wrong, but brute force, glossed over with a little religious hypocrisy and archiepiscopal advice."

Jorgensen, Paul A. *Shakespeare's Military World*, pp. 71–97. Berkeley and Los Angeles: Univ. of California Press, 1956. Jorgensen discusses *Henry V* in the context of his study of Renaissance theories and practice of warfare. Shakespeare "conscientiously followed" Elizabethan military handbooks in his portrait of Henry as a "Christian conqueror," and other aspects of the play similarly reflect Shakespeare's knowledge of Elizabethan military matters.

Kastan, David Scott. " 'The King is a Good King, But it Must Be as it May': History, Heroism, and *Henry V*." *Shakespeare and the Shapes of Time*. Hanover, N.H.: Univ. Press of New England, 1982. For Kastan the play at once acknowledges Henry's heroism as it shapes historical material into patriotic myth and simultaneously recognizes the "instability of the shape of this restructured history." We are made to see Henry as a hero, but we are forced to recognize that his heroism is animated only by his radical simplification of the moral environment of the play.

Kernan, Alvin B. "The Henriad: Shakespeare's Major History Plays." In *Modern Shakespearean Criticism: Essays on Style, Dramaturgy, and the Major Plays*, ed. Alvin B. Kernan. New York: Harcourt, Brace, and World, 1970. Kernan treats *Henry V* as the culmination of a four-part epic moving from Richard II's sacred conception of kingship to Henry's pragmatic understanding of the role. *Henry V*, for Kernan, portrays a successful king, living "in the full glare of public life," who succeeds only by subordinating his private self to his "political function."

Ornstein, Robert. *"Henry V." A Kingdom for a Stage: The Achievement of Shakespeare's History Plays*. Cambridge: Harvard Univ. Press, 1972. Ornstein focuses on Henry's "moral temper": the King is a successful ruler, but one whose "moral awareness is of the mind, not of the heart." Though the play celebrates the heroism of the English, it speaks "candidly of the human cost of their great adventure."

Quinn, Michael, ed. *Shakespeare, "Henry V": A Casebook*. London: Macmillan, 1969. Quinn provides a useful selection of essays, including extracts from early critics such as Samuel Johnson, August Wilhelm von Schlegel, William Hazlitt, and Algernon Swinburne, as well as longer pieces by Derek A. Traversi, Rose Zimbardo, and L. C. Knights.

Rabkin, Norman. "Either / Or: Responding to *Henry V*." *Shakespeare and the Problem of Meaning*. Chicago: Univ. of Chicago Press, 1981. Rabkin finds *Henry V* to be a play that deliberately seeks the ambiguity reflected in the critical debate it has attracted. The play at once celebrates and undermines its hero, revealing "the simultaneity of our deepest hopes and fears about the world of political action."

Reese, M. M. *"Henry V." The Cease of Majesty: A Study of Shakespeare's History Plays*. London: Edward Arnold; New York: St. Martin's Press, 1961. For Reese, Henry is a hero whose undertaking of the French war is right and just and whose success reveals England's recovered strength. Reese argues that the ironies that critics have found are not present in performance; the play provides a "heartening picture of a society cured of its sickness and united under a prince whose own redemptive experience corresponded with that of his people."

Ribner, Irving. "Shakespeare's Second Tetralogy." *The English History Play in the Age of Shakespeare*, 1957. Rev. ed., enl., New York: Barnes and Noble, 1965. Shakespeare's history plays, according to Ribner, reflect the political interests of sixteenth-century historians. *Henry V* is Shakespeare's portrait of an ideal king who displays both the military virtues he had learned in *1 Henry IV* and the civil virtues he had learned in *2 Henry IV*.

Saccio, Peter. "Henry V: The King Victorious." *Shakespeare's English Kings: History, Chronicle, and Drama*. New York: Oxford Univ. Press, 1977. Saccio studies the historical background of Shakespeare's play, examining Henry's claim to the French throne and the "talents and training" that determined his success.

Schlegel, August Wilhelm von. *A Course of Lectures on Dramatic Art and Literature*, trans. John Black, 1846. Rpt., New York: AMS, 1965, pp. 271–367. The argument that Shakespeare's histories "form one great whole," a "heroic poem in the dramatic form," can be traced to Schlegel. Schlegel also argues that Henry "is manifestly Shakespeare's favourite hero in English history," and that the play demonstrates his political maneuverings and personal charm, endowing him "with every chivalrous and kingly virtue."

Traversi, Derek A. *"Henry V." Shakespeare from "Richard II" to "Henry V."* Stanford: Stanford Univ. Press, 1957. Traversi finds in the play "the presence of a subsistent irony" that qualifies the portrait of Henry's success. The effect of Shakespeare's play is "to bring out certain contradictions, moral and human, inherent in the notion of a successful king."

Memorable Lines

O, for a Muse of fire, that would ascend
The brightest heaven of invention!

(CHORUS Prologue.1–2)

Therefore doth heaven divide
The state of man in divers functions,
Setting endeavor in continual motion,
To which is fixèd, as an aim or butt,
Obedience; for so work the honeybees.

(CANTERBURY 1.2.183–187)

The singing masons building roofs of gold . . .

(CANTERBURY 1.2.198)

'Tis ever common
That men are merriest when they are from home.

(HENRY 1.2.271–272)

He's in Arthur's bosom, if ever man went to Arthur's bosom.

(HOSTESS 2.3.9–10)

. . . for his nose was as sharp as a pen, and 'a babbled of green
fields.

(HOSTESS 2.3.16–17)

Trust none,
For oaths are straws, men's faiths are wafer cakes,
And Holdfast is the only dog, my duck.

(PISTOL 2.3.49–51)

Once more unto the breach, dear friends, once more,
Or close the wall up with our English dead!

(HENRY 3.1.1–2)

In peace there's nothing so becomes a man
As modest stillness and humility.
But when the blast of war blows in our ears,
Then imitate the action of the tiger:
Stiffen the sinews, conjure up the blood,

Disguise fair nature with hard-favored rage.
Then lend the eye a terrible aspect. (HENRY 3.1.3–9)

I see you stand like greyhounds in the slips,
Straining upon the start. The game's afoot!
Follow your spirit, and upon this charge
Cry, "God for Harry! England and Saint George!"
(HENRY 3.1.31–34)

I would give all my fame for a pot of ale and safety.
(BOY 3.2.11–12)

Men of few words are the best men. (BOY 3.2.35–36)

MESSENGER My Lord High Constable, the English lie within
fifteen hundred paces of your tents.
CONSTABLE Who hath measured the ground? (3.7.125–127)

. . . that mean and gentle all
Behold, as may unworthiness define,
A little touch of Harry in the night. (CHORUS 4.0.45–47)

There is some soul of goodness in things evil,
Would men observingly distill it out. (HENRY 4.1.4–5)

. . . when blood is their argument . . . (WILLIAMS 4.1.143)

Every subject's duty is the King's; but every subject's soul is
his own. (HENRY 4.1.176–177)

What infinite heartsease
Must kings neglect that private men enjoy!
And what have kings that privates have not too,
Save ceremony, save general ceremony?
(HENRY 4.1.234–237)

O God of battles, steel my soldiers' hearts;
Possess them not with fear! Take from them now
The sense of reckoning, ere th' opposèd numbers
Pluck their hearts from them. (HENRY 4.1.287–290)

But if it be a sin to covet honor
I am the most offending soul alive.   (HENRY   4.3.28–29)

We few, we happy few, we band of brothers.
For he today that sheds his blood with me
Shall be my brother.   (HENRY   4.3.60–62)

Doth Fortune play the huswife with me now?
(PISTOL   5.1.79)

To England will I steal, and there I'll steal;
And patches will I get unto these cudgeled scars,
And swear I got them in the Gallia wars.   (PISTOL   5.1.86–88)

Even so our houses and ourselves and children
Have lost, or do not learn for want of time,
The sciences that should become our country,
But grow like savages.   (BURGUNDY   5.2.56–59)

HENRY   Canst thou love me?
KATHARINE   I cannot tell.
HENRY   Can any of your neighbors tell, Kate?   (5.2.195–197)

Your Majestee 'ave *fausse* French enough to deceive de most
sage demoiselle dat is *en France*.   (KATHARINE   5.2.219–220)

Nice customs curtsy to great kings.   (HENRY   5.2.271)

Small time, but in that small most greatly lived
This Star of England.   (CHORUS   Epilogue.5–6)

Contributors

DAVID BEVINGTON, Phyllis Fay Horton Professor of Humanities at the University of Chicago, is editor of *The Complete Works of Shakespeare* (Scott, Foresman, 1980) and of *Medieval Drama* (Houghton Mifflin, 1975). His latest critical study is *Action Is Eloquence: Shakespeare's Language of Gesture* (Harvard University Press, 1984).

DAVID SCOTT KASTAN, Professor of English and Comparative Literature at Columbia University, is the author of *Shakespeare and the Shapes of Time* (University Press of New England, 1982).

JAMES HAMMERSMITH, Associate Professor of English at Auburn University, has published essays on various facets of Renaissance drama, including literary criticism, textual criticism, and printing history.

ROBERT KEAN TURNER, Professor of English at the University of Wisconsin–Milwaukee, is a general editor of the New Variorum Shakespeare (Modern Language Association of America) and a contributing editor to *The Dramatic Works in the Beaumont and Fletcher Canon* (Cambridge University Press, 1966–).

JAMES SHAPIRO, who coedited the bibliographies with David Scott Kastan, is Assistant Professor of English at Columbia University.

✤

JOSEPH PAPP, one of the most important forces in theater today, is the founder and producer of the New York Shakespeare Festival, America's largest and most prolific theatrical institution. Since 1954 Mr. Papp has produced or directed all but one of Shakespeare's plays—in Central Park, in schools, off and on Broadway, and at the Festival's permanent home, The Public Theater. He has also produced such award-winning plays and musical works as *Hair, A Chorus Line, Plenty,* and *The Mystery of Edwin Drood,* among many others.

THE BANTAM SHAKESPEARE COLLECTION

The Complete Works in 28 Volumes

Edited with Introductions by David Bevington

Forewords by Joseph Papp

___ANTONY AND CLEOPATRA	21289-3	$3.95
___AS YOU LIKE IT	21290-7	$3.95
___A COMEDY OF ERRORS	21291-5	$3.95
___HAMLET	21292-3	$3.95
___HENRY IV, PART I	21293-1	$3.95
___HENRY IV, PART II	21294-X	$3.95
___HENRY V	21295-8	$3.95
___JULIUS CAESAR	21296-6	$3.95
___KING LEAR	21297-4	$3.95
___MACBETH	21298-2	$3.95
___THE MERCHANT OF VENICE	21299-0	$2.95
___A MIDSUMMER NIGHT'S DREAM	21300-8	$3.95
___MUCH ADO ABOUT NOTHING	21301-6	$3.95
___OTHELLO	21302-4	$3.95
___RICHARD II	21303-2	$3.95
___RICHARD III	21304-0	$3.95
___ROMEO AND JULIET	21305-9	$3.95
___THE TAMING OF THE SHREW	21306-7	$3.95
___THE TEMPEST	21307-5	$3.95
___TWELFTH NIGHT	21308-3	$3.50
___FOUR COMEDIES *(The Taming of the Shrew, A Midsummer Night's Dream, The Merchant of Venice,* and *Twelfth Night)*	21281-8	$4.95
___THREE EARLY COMEDIES *(Love's Labor's Lost, The Two Gentlemen of Verona,* and *The Merry Wives of Windsor)*	21282-6	$4.95
___FOUR TRAGEDIES *(Hamlet, Othello, King Lear,* and *Macbeth)*	21283-4	$5.95
___HENRY VI, PARTS I, II, and III	21285-0	$4.95
___KING JOHN and HENRY VIII	21286-9	$4.95
___MEASURE FOR MEASURE, ALL'S WELL THAT ENDS WELL, and TROILUS AND CRESSIDA	21287-7	$4.95
___THE LATE ROMANCES *(Pericles, Cymbeline, The Winter's Tale,* and *The Tempest)*	21288-5	$4.95
___THE POEMS	21309-1	$4.95

the BANTAM Shakespeare

Bantam is proud to announce an important new
edition of:

The Complete Works Of
William Shakespeare

Featuring:

*The complete texts with modern spelling and
punctuation

*Vivid, readable introductions by noted Shakespearean
  scholar David Bevington
*New forewords by Joseph Papp, renowned producer,
  director, and founder of the New York Shakespeare
  Festival
*Stunning, original cover art by Mark English, the
  most awarded illustrator in the history of the Society
  of Illustrators
*Photographs from some of the most celebrated
  performances by the New York Shakespeare Festival
*Complete source materials, notes, and annotated
  bibliographies based on the latest scholarships
*Stage histories for each play

ACCESSIBLE * AUTHORITATIVE * COMPLETE

SHAKESPEARE
The Complete works in 29 Volumes